CSS
Pocket Reference

SECOND EDITION

CSS
Pocket Reference

Eric A. Meyer

O'REILLY®

Beijing · Cambridge · Farnham · Köln · Paris · Sebastopol · Taipei · Tokyo

CSS Pocket Reference, Second Edition

by Eric A. Meyer

Copyright © 2004, 2001 O'Reilly Media, Inc. All rights reserved.
Printed in the United States of America.

Published by O'Reilly Media, Inc., 1005 Gravenstein Highway North,
Sebastopol, CA 95472.

O'Reilly books may be purchased for educational, business, or sales
promotional use. Online editions are also available for most titles
(*safari.oreilly.com*). For more information, contact our corporate/
institutional sales department: (800) 998-9938 or *corporate@oreilly.com*.

Editors:	Molly Wood and Tatiana Apandi Diaz
Production Editor:	Colleen Gorman
Cover Designer:	Ellie Volckhausen
Interior Designer:	Melanie Wang

Printing History:

May 2001:	First Edition.
July 2004:	Second Edition.

0-596-00777-9
[C]

Contents

CSS Pocket Reference

Cascading Style Sheets (CSS) is the W3C standard for the visual presentation of web pages (although it can be used in other settings as well). After a short introduction to the key concepts of CSS, this pocket reference provides an alphabetical reference to all CSS2.1 selectors, followed by an alphabetical reference for all CSS2.1 properties.

Conventions Used in This Book

The following typographical conventions are used in this book:

Italic

> Used to indicate new terms, URLs, filenames, file extensions, directories, commands and options, and program names. For example, a path in the filesystem will appear as *C:\windows\system*.

`Constant width`

> Used to show the contents of files or the output from commands.

For more information, visit O'Reilly's web site for this book, where examples, errata, and any plans for future editions are listed:

> *http://www.oreilly.com/catalog/csspr2*

Adding Styles to HTML and XHTML

Styles can be applied to documents in three distinct ways, as discussed in the following sections.

Inline Styles

In HTML and XHTML, style information can be specified for an individual element via the style attribute. The value of a style attribute is a declaration block without the curly brackets.

```
<p style="color: red; background: yellow;">Look out!
This text is alarmingly presented!</p>
```

Note that, as of this writing, a full style sheet cannot be placed into a style attribute. For example, it is not possible to place hover styles (using :hover) in a style attribute.

Although typical XML document languages (e.g., XHTML 1.0, XHTML 1.1, and SVG) support the style attribute, it is unlikely that all XML languages will support a similar capability. Due to this and the fact that it encourages poor authoring practices, authors are generally discouraged from using the style attribute.

Embedded Style Sheets

A style sheet can be embedded at the top of an HTML or XHTML document using the style element, which must appear within the head element.

```
<html><head><title>Stylin'!</title>
<style type="text/css">
h1 {color: purple;}
p {font-size: smaller; color: gray;}
</style>
</head>
   ...
</html>
```

XML languages may or may not provide an equivalent capability; always check the language DTD to be certain.

External Style Sheets

Styles can be listed in a separate file. The primary advantage to a separate file is that by collecting commonly used styles in a single file, all pages that use that style sheet can be updated by editing a single style sheet. Another key advantage is that external style sheets are cached, which can help reduce bandwidth usage. An external style sheet can be referenced in one of the following three ways.

@import directive

One or more @import directives can be placed at the beginning of any style sheet. Inside an HTML and XHTML document, this would be done within an embedded style sheet.

```
<head>
<title>My Document</title>
<style type="text/css">
@import url(site.css);
@import url(navbar.css);
@import url(footer.css);
body {background: yellow;}
</style>
</head>
```

Note that @import directives can appear at the top of any style sheet. Thus, one style sheet could import another, which in turn imports a third.

link element

In HTML and XHTML documents, the link element can be used to associate a style sheet with the document. Multiple link elements are permitted. The media attribute can be used to restrict a style sheet to one or more media.

```
<head>
<title>A Document</title>
<link rel="stylesheet" type="text/css" href="basic.css"
```

```
    media="all">
<link rel="stylesheet" type="text/css" href="web.css"
  media="screen">
<link rel="stylesheet" type="text/css" href="paper.css"
  media="print">
</head>
```

It is also possible to link to alternate style sheets. If alternate style sheets are supplied, it is up to the user agent (or the author) to provide a means for the user to select one of the alternates.

```
<head>
<title>A Document</title>
<link rel="stylesheet" type="text/css" href="basic.css">
<link rel="alternate stylesheet" title="Classic"
type="text/css" href="oldschool.css">
<link rel="alternate stylesheet" title="Futuristic"
type="text/css" href="3000ad.css">
</head>
```

As of this writing, most or all known user agents load all linked style sheets, including the alternate style sheets, regardless of whether the user ever uses them. This can have implications for bandwidth use and server load.

xml-stylesheet processing instruction

In XML documents (such as XHTML documents sent with a mime-type of "text/xml", "application/xml", or "application/xhtml+xml"), the xml-stylesheet processing instruction can be used to associate a style sheet with the document. Any xml-stylesheet processing instructions must be placed in the prolog of an XML document. Multiple xml-stylesheet processing instructions are permitted. The media pseudo-attribue can be used to restrict a style sheet to one or more forms of media.

```
<?xml-stylesheet type="text/css" href="basic.css"
  media="all"?>
<?xml-stylesheet type="text/css" href="web.css"
  media="screen"?>
<?xml-stylesheet type="text/css" href="paper.css"
  media="print"?>
```

It is also possible to link to alternate style sheets with the xml-stylesheet processing instruction

```
<?xml-stylesheet type="text/css" href="basic.css"?>
<?xml-stylesheet alternate="yes" title="Classic"
  type="text/css" href="oldschool.css"?>
<?xml-stylesheet alternate="yes" title="Futuristic"
  type="text/css" href="3000ad.css"?>
```

Rule Structure

A style sheet consists of one of more rules that describe how page elements should be presented. Every rule has two fundamental parts: the *selector* and the *declaration block*. Figure 1 illustrates the structure of a rule.

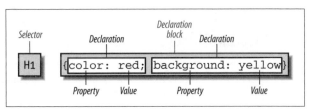

Figure 1. Rule structure

On the left side of the rule, we find the selector, which selects the parts of the document to which the rule should be applied. On the right side of the rule, we have the declaration block. A declaration block is made up of one or more *declarations*; each declaration is a combination of a CSS *property* and a *value* of that property.

The declaration block is always enclosed in curly brackets. A declaration block can contain several declarations; each declaration must be terminated with a semicolon (;). The exception is the final declaration in a declaration block, for which the semicolon is optional.

Each property, which represents a particular stylistic parameter, is separated from its value by a colon (:). Property names in CSS are not case-sensitive. Legal values for a property are defined by the property description. The "Property Reference" section, later in this book, provides details on acceptable values for CSS properties.

Style Precedence

A single HTML document can import and link to multiple external style sheets, contain one or more embedded style sheets, and make use of inline styles. In the process, it is quite possible that some rules will conflict with each other. CSS uses a mechanism called the *cascade* to resolve any such conflicts and arrive at a final set of styles to be applied to the document. Two key components of the cascade are *specificity* and *inheritance*.

Specificity Calculations

Specificity describes the weight of a selector and any declarations associated with that selector. The following chart summarizes the components of specificity summation.

Selector type	Specificity
Universal selector Combinators	0,0,0,0
Element identifier Pseudo-element identifier	0,0,0,1
Class identifier Pseudo-class identifier Attribute identifier	0,0,1,0
ID identifier	0,1,0,0
Inline style	1,0,0,0

Specificity values are cumulative. Thus, a selector containing two element identifiers and a class identifier (e.g., div.aside p) has a specificity of 0,0,1,2. Specificity values are sorted in right-to-left precedence; thus, a selector containing eleven element identifiers (0,0,0,11) is of lower specificity than a selector containing just a single class identifier (0,0,1,0).

The !important directive gives a declaration more weight than nonimportant declarations. The declaration retains the specificity of its selectors, and is used only in comparison with other important declarations.

Inheritance

The elements in a document form a tree-like hierarchy with the root element at the top and the rest of the document structure spreading out below it (which makes it look more like a tree root system, really). In an HTML document, the html element is at the top of the tree, with the head and body elements descending from it. From those elements descend the rest of the document structure. In such a structure, elements lower down in the tree are descendants of the ancestors, which are higher in the tree.

CSS uses the document tree for the mechanism of *inheritance*, in which a style applied to an element is inherited by its descendants. For example, if the body element is set to have a color of red, that value propagates down the document tree to the elements that descend from the body element. This inheritance is interrupted only by a style rule that applies directly to an element. Inherited values have no specificity at all (which is *not* the same as having zero specificity).

Note that some elements are not inherited. A property will always define whether it is inherited. Some examples of non-inherited properties are padding, border, margin, and background.

The Cascade

The cascade is how CSS resolves conflicts between styles; it is, in other words, the mechanism by which a user agent decides, for example, what color to make an element when two different rules apply to it and each one tries to set a different color. The following steps constitute the cascade:

1. Find all declarations that contain a selector that matches a given element.

2. Sort by explicit weight all declarations applying to the element. Those rules marked !important are given greater weight than those that are not. Also, sort by origin all declarations applying to a given element. There are three origins: author, reader, and user agent. Under normal circumstances, the author's styles win out over the reader's styles. !important reader styles are stronger than any other styles, including !important author styles. Both author and reader styles override the user agent's default styles.

3. Sort by specificity all declarations applying to a given element. Those elements with a higher specificity have more weight than those with lower specificity.

4. Sort by order all declarations applying to a given element. The later a declaration appears in the style sheet or document, the more weight it is given. Declarations that appear in an imported style sheet are considered to come before all declarations within the style sheet that imports them.

Element Classification

Broadly speaking, CSS groups elements into two types: *replaced* and *nonreplaced*. Although the types may seem rather abstract, there actually are some differences in how the two kinds of element are presented. These differences are explored in detail in Chapter 7 of *Cascading Style Sheets: The Definitive Guide*, Second Edition (O'Reilly).

Nonreplaced Elements

The majority of HTML and XHTML elements are *nonreplaced elements*. This means their content is presented by the user agent inside a box generated by the element itself. For example, `<span>hi there</span>` is a nonreplaced element, and the text `hi there` will be displayed by the user agent. Paragraphs, headings, table cells, lists, and almost everything else in XHTML are nonreplaced elements.

Replaced Elements

In contrast, *replaced elements* are those where the element's content is replaced by something not directly represented by document content. The most familiar XHTML example is the `img` element, which is replaced by an image file external to the document itself. In fact, `img` has no actual content, as we can see by considering a simple example.

```
<img src="howdy.gif" alt="Hi" />
```

There is no content contained in the element—only an element name and attributes. Only by replacing the element's lack of content with content found through other means (in this case, loading an external image specified by the `src` attribute) can the element have any presentation at all. Another example is the `input` element, which may be replaced with a radio button, checkbox, or text input box, depending on its type. Replaced elements also generate boxes in their display.

Element Display Roles

In addition to being replaced or not, there are two basic types of element display roles in CSS2: *block-level* and *inline-level*.

Block-Level

Block-level elements are those that generate an element box that (by default) fills its parent element's content area, and cannot have other elements to its sides. In other words, block-level elements generate "breaks" before and after the element box. The most familiar block elements from HTML are p and div. Replaced elements can be block-level elements, but usually are not.

List items are a special case of block-level elements. In addition to behaving in a manner consistent with other block elements, they generate a marker—typically a bullet for unordered lists or a number for ordered lists—which is "attached" to the element box. Except for the presence of this marker, list items are in all other ways identical to other block elements.

Inline-Level Elements

Inline-level elements are those that generate an element box within a line of text and do not break up the flow of that line. The best inline element example is the a element in XHTML. Other candidates would be strong and em. These elements do not generate a break before or after themselves and so can appear within the content of another element without disrupting its display.

Note that while the CSS block and inline elements have a great deal in common with HTML and XHTML block- and inline-level elements, there is an important difference: in HTML and XHTML, block-level elements cannot descend from inline-level elements, whereas in CSS, there is no restriction on how display roles can be nested within each other.

Basic Visual Layout

CSS defines algorithms for laying out any element in a document. These algorithms form the underpinnings of visual presentation in CSS. There are two primary kinds of layout, each with very different behaviors: block-level and inline-level layout.

Block-Level Layout

A block-level box in CSS generates a rectangular box called the *element box*. This box describes the amount of space occupied by an element. Figure 2 shows the various components of an element box. The following rules apply to an element box:

- The background of an element extends to the outer edge of the border, thus filling the content, padding, and border areas. If the border has any transparent portions (e.g, it is dotted or dashed), then the background will be visible in those portions.

- Only the margins, height, and width of an element box may be set to auto.

- Only margins can be given negative length values.

- The padding and borders of the element box default to 0 (zero) and none, respectively.

- The property width defines only the width of the content area; any padding, borders, or margins are added to it. The same is true for height.

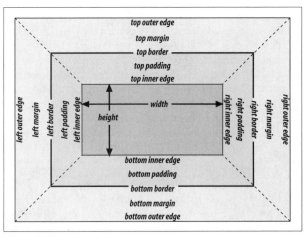

Figure 2. Box model details

Inline Layout

All inline elements have a `line-height`, which has a great deal to do with how the elements are displayed. The height of a line of text is determined by taking into account the following factors:

Anonymous text

Any string of characters not contained within an inline element. Thus, in the markup:

```
<p> I'm <em>so</em> happy!</p>
```

the sequences " I'm " and " happy!" are anonymous text. Note that the spaces are part of that text, since a space is a character like any other.

Em-box

The em-box defined in the given font; otherwise known as the character box. Actual glyphs can be taller or shorter than their em-boxes, as discussed in Chapter 5 of *Cascading Style Sheets: The Definitive Guide*, Second Edition. In CSS, the value of `font-size` determines the height of each em-box.

Content area

In nonreplaced elements, the content area can be the box described by the em-boxes of every character in the element, strung together, or else the box described by the character glyphs in the element. The CSS2.1 specification allows user agents to choose either. This text uses the em-box definition, for simplicity's sake. In replaced elements, the content area is the intrinsic height of the element plus any margins, borders, or padding.

Leading

The leading is the difference between the values of `font-size` and `line-height`. Half this difference is applied to the top and half to the bottom of the content area. These additions to the content area are called, not

---

surprisingly, half-leading. Leading is applied only to non-replaced elements.

Inline box

The box described by the addition of the leading to the content area. For nonreplaced elements, the height of the inline box of an element will be equal to the value for `line-height`. For replaced elements, the height of the inline box of an element will be equal to the content area, since leading is not applied to replaced elements.

Line box

The shortest box that bounds the highest and lowest points of the inline boxes that are found in the line. In other words, the top edge of the line box will be placed along the top of the highest inline box top, and the bottom of the line box is placed along the bottom of the lowest inline box bottom. (See Figure 3.)

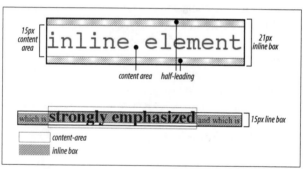

Figure 3. Inline layout details

Floating Rules

Floating allows an element to be placed to the left or right of its containing block (which is the nearest block-level ancestor element), with following content flowing around the element. A floated element is placed according to the following rules:

1. The left (or right) outer edge of a floated element may not be to the left (or right) of the inner edge of its containing block.

2. The left (or right) outer edge of a floated element must be to the right (or left) of the right (left) outer edge of a left-floating (or right-floating) element that occurs earlier in the document's source, unless the top of the later element is below the bottom of the former.

3. The right outer edge of a left-floating element may not be to the right of the left outer edge of any right-floating element to its right. The left outer edge of a right-floating element may not be to the left of the right outer edge of any left-floating element to its left.

4. A floating element's top may not be higher than the inner top of its containing block.

5. A floating element's top may not be higher than the top of any earlier floating or block-level element.

6. A floating element's top may not be higher than the top of any line box with content that precedes the floating element.

7. A left (or right) floating element that has another floating element to its left (right) may not have its right outer edge to the right (left) of its containing block's right (left) edge.

8. A floating element must be placed as high as possible.

9. A left-floating element must be put as far to the left as possible, a right-floating element as far to the right as possible. A higher position is preferred to one that is further to the right or left.

Positioning Rules

When elements are positioned, a number of special rules come into play. These rules govern not only the containing block of the element, but also how it is laid out within that element.

Types of Positioning

Static positioning
> The element's box is generated as normal. Block-level elements generate a rectangular box that is part of the document's flow, and inline-level boxes generate one or more line boxes that flow within their parent element.

Relative positioning
> The element's box is offset by some distance. Its containing block can be considered to be the area that the element would occupy if it were not positioned. The element retains the shape it would have had were it not positioned, and the space that the element would ordinarily have occupied is preserved.

Absolute positioning
> The element's box is completely removed from the flow of the document and positioned with respect to its containing block, which may be another element in the document or the initial containing block (described in the next section). Whatever space the element might have occupied in the normal document flow is closed up, as though the element did not exist. The positioned element generates a block box, regardless of the type of box it would generate if it were in the normal flow.

Fixed positioning
> The element's box behaves as though it were set to absolute, but its containing block is the viewport itself.

The Containing Block

The containing block of a positioned element is determined as follows:

1. The containing block of the *root element* (also called the *initial containing block*) is established by the user agent. In HTML, the root element is the html element, although some browsers may use body.

2. For nonroot elements, if the element's position value is relative or static, the containing block is formed by the content edge of the nearest block-level, table-, cell-, or inline-block ancestor box. (Despite this rule, relatively positioned elements are still simply offset, not positioned with respect to the containing block described here.)

3. For nonroot elements that have a position value of absolute, the containing block is set to the nearest ancestor (of any kind) that has a position value other than static. This happens as follows:

    a. If the ancestor is block-level, the containing block is that element's padding edge; in other words, it is the area that would be bounded by a border.

    b. If the ancestor is inline-level, the containing block is set to the content edge of the ancestor. In left-to-right languages, the top and left of the containing block are the top and left content edges of the first box in the ancestor, and the bottom and right edges are the bottom and right content edges of the last box. In right-to-left languages, the right edge of the containing block corresponds to the right content edge of the first box, and the left is taken from the last box. The top and bottom are the same.

    c. If there are no ancestors as described in a) and b), then the element's containing block is defined to be the initial containing block.

Layout of Absolutely Positioned Elements

In the following sections, these terms are used:

Shrink-to-fit
> Similar to calculating the width of a table cell using the automatic table layout algorithm. In general, the user agent attempts to find the minimum element width that will contain the content and will wrap to multiple lines only if wrapping cannot be avoided.

Static position
> The place where an element's edge would have been placed if its position were static.

Horizontal layout of nonreplaced absolutely positioned elements

The equation that governs the layout of these elements is:

```
left + margin-left + border-left-width + padding-left +
width + padding-right + border-right-width + margin-right
+ right = width of containing block
```

The steps used to determine layout are:

1. If all of left, width, and right are auto, first reset any auto values for margin-left and margin-right to 0. Then, if direction is ltr, set left to the static position and apply the third rule in the list given in step 3. Otherwise, set right to the static position and apply the first rule in the list given in step 3.

2. If none of left, width, and right are auto, pick the rule that applies from the following list:

    a. If both margin-left and margin-right are set to auto, solve the equation under the additional constraint that the two margins get equal values.

    b. If only one of margin-left or margin-right is set to auto, solve the equation for that value.

    c. If the values are overconstrained (none are set to auto), ignore the value for `left` (if `direction` is `rtl`; ignore `right` if `direction` is `ltr`) and solve for that value.

3. If some of `left`, `width`, and `right` are auto, but others are not, reset any auto values for `margin-left` and `margin-right` to 0. From the following list, pick the one rule that applies:

    a. If `left` and `width` are auto and `right` is not auto, then the width is shrink-to-fit. Solve the equation for `left`.

    b. If `left` and `right` are auto and `width` is not auto, then if `direction` is `ltr`, set `left` to the static position (otherwise, set `right` to the static position). Solve the equation for `left` (if `direction` is `rtl`) or `right` (if `direction` is `ltr`).

    c. If `width` and `right` are auto and `left` is not auto, then the width is shrink-to-fit. Solve the question for `right`.

    d. If `left` is auto, and `width` and `right` are not auto, solve the equation for `left`.

    e. If `width` is auto, and `left` and `right` are not auto, solve the equation for `width`.

    f. If `right` is auto, and `left` and `width` are not auto, solve the equation for `right`.

Vertical layout of nonreplaced absolutely positioned elements

The equation that governs the layout of these elements is:

```
top + margin-top + border-top-width + padding-top + height
+ padding-bottom + border-bottom-width + margin-bottom +
bottom = height of containing block
```

The steps used to determine layout are:

1. If all of `top`, `height`, and `bottom` are auto, set `top` to the static position and apply the third rule in the list given in step 3.

---

2. If none of `top`, `height`, and `bottom` are `auto`, pick the one rule that applies from the following list:

   a. If both `margin-top` and `margin-bottom` are set to `auto`, solve the equation under the additional constraint that the two margins get equal values.

   b. If only one of `margin-top` or `margin-bottom` is set to `auto`, solve the equation for that value.

   c. If the values are overconstrained (none are set to `auto`), ignore the value for `bottom` and solve for that value.

3. If some of `top`, `height`, and `bottom` are `auto`, but others are not, pick the one rule that applies from the following list:

   a. If `top` and `height` are `auto` and `bottom` is not `auto`, then the height is based on the element's content (as it would be in the static flow). Reset any `auto` values for `margin-top` and `margin-bottom` to 0 and solve the equation for `top`.

   b. If `top` and `bottom` are `auto` and `height` is not `auto`, then set `top` to the static position. Reset any `auto` values for `margin-top` and `margin-bottom` to 0 and solve the equation for `bottom`.

   c. If `height` and `bottom` are `auto` and `top` is not `auto`, then the height is based on the element's content (as it would be in the static flow). Reset any `auto` values for `margin-top` and `margin-bottom` to 0 and solve the equation for `bottom`.

   d. If `top` is `auto`, and `height` and `bottom` are not `auto`, reset any `auto` values for `margin-top` and `margin-bottom` to 0 and solve the equation for `top`.

   e. If `height` is `auto`, and `top` and `bottom` are not `auto`, reset any `auto` values for `margin-top` and `margin-bottom` to 0 and solve the equation for `height`.

   f. If `bottom` is `auto`, and `top` and `height` are not `auto`, reset any `auto` values for `margin-top` and `margin-bottom` to 0 and solve the equation for `bottom`.

Horizontal layout of replaced absolutely positioned elements

The behaviors that go into placing and sizing replaced elements are most easily expressed as a series of rules to be taken one after the other. These rules state:

1. If width is set to auto, the computed value of width is determined by the intrinsic width of the element's content. Thus, the width of an image 50 pixels wide is computed to be 50px. If width is explicitly declared (that is, something like 100px or 50%), then the width is set to that value.

2. If left has the value auto in a left-to-right language, replace auto with the static position. In right-to-left languages, replace an auto value for right with the static position.

3. If either left or right is still auto (in other words, it hasn't been replaced in a previous step), replace any auto value in margin-left or margin-right with 0.

4. If at this point both margin-left and margin-right are still defined to be auto, set them to be equal, thus centering the element in its containing block.

5. After all that, if there is only one auto value left, change it to equal the remainder of the equation.

Vertical layout of replaced absolutely positioned elements

The behaviors that go into placing and sizing replaced elements are most easily expressed as a series of rules to be taken one after the other. These state:

1. If height is set to auto, the computed value of height is determined by the intrinsic height of the element's content. Thus, the height of an image 50 pixels tall is computed to be 50px. If height is explicitly declared (that is, something like 100px or 50%), then the height is set to that value.

2. If top has the value auto, replace the value with the replaced element's static position.

3. If bottom has a value of auto, replace any auto value on margin-top or margin-bottom with 0.

4. If at this point both margin-top and margin-bottom are still defined to be auto, set them to be equal, thus centering the element in its containing block.

5. After all that, if there is only one auto value left, change it to equal the remainder of the equation.

Table Layout

The layout of tables can get quite complicated, especially since CSS defines two different ways to calculate table and cell widths, as well as two ways to handle the borders of tables and elements internal to the table. Figure 4 illustrates the components of a table.

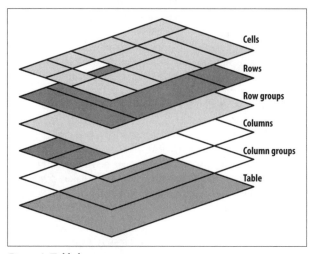

Figure 4. Table layout components

Table Arrangement Rules

In general, a table is laid out according to the following principles:

1. Each row box encompasses a single row of grid cells. All of the row boxes in a table fill the table from top to bottom in the order they occur in the source document. Thus, the table contains as many grid rows as there are row elements.

2. A row group's box encompasses the same grid cells as the row boxes that it contains.

3. A column box encompasses one or more columns of grid cells. Column boxes are placed next to each other in the order they occur. The first column box is on the left for left-to-right languages and on the right for right-to-left languages.

4. A column group's box encompasses the same grid cells as the column boxes that it contains.

5. Although cells may span several rows or columns, CSS does not define how this happens. It is instead left to the document language to define spanning. Each spanned cell is a rectangular box one or more grid cells wide and high. The top row of this rectangle is in the row that is parent to the cell. The cell's rectangle must be as far to the left as possible in left-to-right languages, but it may not overlap any other cell box. It must also be to the right of all cells in the same row that are earlier in the source document in a left-to-right language. In right-to-left languages, a spanned cell must be as far to the right as possible without overlapping other cells, and must be to the left of all cells in the same row that come after it in the document source.

6. A cell's box cannot extend beyond the last row box of a table or row group. If the table structure causes this condition, the cell must be shortened until it fits within the table or row group that encloses it.

Fixed Table Layout

The fixed-layout model is fast because its layout doesn't depend on the contents of table cells; it's driven by the `width` values of the table, columns and cells within the first row of that table. The fixed-layout model uses the following simple steps:

1. Any column element whose `width` property has a value other than `auto` sets the width for that column.

2. If a column has an `auto` width, but the cell in the first row of the table within that column has a `width` other than `auto`, then that cell sets the width for that column. If the cell spans multiple columns, then the width is divided equally among the columns.

3. Any columns that are still auto-sized are sized so that their widths are as equal as possible.

At that point, the width of the table is set to be either the value of `width` for the table or the sum of the column widths, whichever is greater. If the table turns out to be wider than the column widths, the difference is divided by the number of columns and added to each of them.

Automatic Table Layout

The automatic-layout model, while not as fast as fixed-layout, is likely to be much more familiar to authors, because it's substantially the same model that HTML tables have used for years. In most current user agents, use of this model will be triggered by a table with a `width` of `auto`, regardless of the value of `table-layout`—although this is not assured.

The details of the model can be expressed in the following steps:

1. For each cell in a column, calculate both the minimum and maximum cell width.

2. Determine the minimum width required to display the content. In determining this minimum content width,

the content can flow to any number of lines, but it may not stick out of the cell's box. If the cell has a width value that is larger than the minimum possible width, then the minimum cell width is set to the value of width. If the cell's width value is auto, then the minimum cell width is set to the minimum content width.

3. For the maximum width, determine the width required to display the content without any line-breaking, other than that forced by explicit line-breaking (e.g., due to the <br> element). That value is the maximum cell width.

4. For each column, calculate both the minimum and maximum column width.

   a. The column's minimum width is determined by the largest minimum cell width of the cells within the column. If the column has been given an explicit width value that is larger than any of the minimum cell widths within the column, then the minimum column width is set to the value of width.

   b. For the maximum width, take the largest maximum cell width of the cells within the column. If the column has been given an explicit width value that is larger than any of the maximum cell widths within the column, then the maximum column width is set to the value of width. These two behaviors recreate the traditional HTML table behavior of forcibly expanding any column to be as wide as its widest cell.

5. In cases where a cell spans more than one column, the sum of the minimum column widths must be equal to the minimum cell width for the spanning cell. Similarly, the sum of the maximum column widths must equal the spanning cell's maximum width. User agents should divide any changes in column widths equally among the spanned columns.

In addition, the user agent must take into account that when a column width has a percentage value for its width, the percentage is calculated in relation to the width of the table—even though that width is not yet known. The user agent must hang on to the percentage value and use it in the next part of the algorithm. Once the user agent has determined how wide or narrow each column can be, it can then calculate the width of the table. This happens as follows:

1. If the computed width of the table is not auto, then the computed table width is compared to the sum of all the column widths plus any borders and cell-spacing. (Columns with percentage widths are likely calculated at this time.) The larger of the two values is the final width of the table. If the table's computed width is larger than the sum of the column widths, borders, and cell-spacing, then all columns are increased in width by an equal amount so they fill the computed width of the table.

2. If the computed width of the table is auto, then the final width of the table is determined by summing up the column widths, borders, and cell-spacing. This means the table will be only as wide as needed to display its content, just as with traditional HTML tables. Any columns with percentage widths use that percentage as a constraint, but it is a constraint that a user agent does not have to satisfy.

Once the last step is completed, then (and only then) can the user agent actually lay out the table.

Collapsing Cell Borders

The collapsing cell model largely describes how HTML tables have always been laid out when they have no cell-spacing. The rules that govern this model are:

- Table elements cannot have any padding, although they can have margins. Thus, there is never separation between the border around the outside of the table and its outermost cells.

- Borders can be applied to cells, rows, row groups, columns, and column groups. The `table` element itself can, as always, have a border.

- There is never any separation between cell borders. In fact, borders collapse into each other where they adjoin, so that only one of the collapsing borders is actually drawn. This is somewhat akin to margin-collapsing, where the largest margin wins. When cell borders collapse, the "most interesting" border wins.

- Once they are collapsed, the borders between cells are centered on the hypothetical grid lines between the cells.

Collapsing borders

When two or more borders are adjacent, they collapse into each other, as shown in Figure 5. There are some strict rules governing which borders will win, and which will not.

1. If one of the collapsing borders has a `border-style` of `hidden`, it takes precedence over all other collapsing borders: all borders at this location are hidden.

2. If one of the collapsing borders has a `border-style` of `none`, it takes the lowest priority. There will be no border drawn at this location only if the all of the borders meeting at this location have a value of `none`. Note that `none` is the default value for `border-style`.

3. If at least one of the collapsing borders has a value other than either `none` or `hidden`, then narrow borders lose out to wider ones. If two or more of the collapsing borders have the same width, then the border style is taken in the following order, from most- to least-preferred: `double`, `solid`, `dashed`, `dotted`, `ridge`, `outset`, `groove`, `inset`. Thus, if two borders with the same width collapse and one is `dashed` while the other is `outset`, the border at that location will be dashed.

---

4. If collapsing borders have the same style and width but differ in color, the color used is taken from an element in the following list, from most preferred to least: cell, row, row group, column, column group, table. Thus, if the borders of a cell and a column, identical in every way except color, collapse, then the cell's border color (and style and width) will be used. If the collapsing borders come from the same type of element—such as two row borders with the same style and width, but different colors—then the behavior is not defined; it is left up to each user agent to decide what to do in such cases.

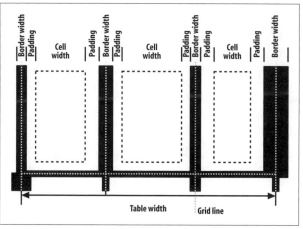

Figure 5. Collapsing cell borders model

Vertical Alignment Within Cells

The following describes the detailed process for aligning cell contents within a row:

1. If any of the cells are baseline-aligned, then the row's baseline is determined and the content of the baseline-aligned cells is placed.

2. Any top-aligned cell has its content placed. The row now has a provisional height, which is defined by the lowest cell bottom of the cells that have already had their content placed.

3. If any remaining cells are middle- or bottom-aligned, and the content height is taller than the provisional row height, the height of the row is increased to enclose the tallest of those cells.

4. All remaining cells have their content placed. In any cell with contents shorter than the row height, the cell's padding is increased in order to match the height of the row.

Values

There are a variety of value types in CSS, most of which use units. By combining basic value types (such as numbers) with units (such as pixels), it becomes possible to do any number of interesting things with CSS.

Keywords

Keywords are defined on a per-property basis and have a meaning specific only to a given property. For example, normal has totally unique meanings for the properties font-variant and letter-spacing. Keywords, like property names, are not case-sensitive. A special case is the keyword inherit, which is allowed on all properties and always has the same meaning (get the property value from the element's parent).

Color Values

#RRGGBB

This is a hex-pair notation familiar to authors using traditional HTML. In this format, the first pair of digits corresponds to the red setting, the second pair to green, and the third pair to blue. Each pair is in hexadecimal notation in the range 00 – FF. Thus, a "pure" blue would be written #0000FF, "pure" red is written #FF0000, and so on.

#RGB

This is a shorter form of the six-digit notation described above. In this format, each digit is replicated to arrive at an equivalent six-digit value; thus, #F8C becomes #FF88CC.

rgb(rrr.rr%,ggg.gg%,bbb.bb%)

This format allows the author to use RGB values in the range 0% to 100%, with decimal values allowed (e.g., 75.5%). The value for black would thus be rgb(0%,0%,0%), whereas "pure" blue would be rgb(0%,0%,100%).

rgb(rrr,ggg,bbb)

Similar to the previous value, the difference here is that the accepted range of values is 0–255. Not coincidentally, this range is the decimal equivalent of 00–FF in hexadecimal. In this format, "pure" green would be rgb(0,255,0), and white would be represented as rgb(255,255,255).

<keyword>

One of 17 recognized keywords based largely on the original Windows VGA colors. These keywords are: aqua, black, blue, fuchsia, gray, green, lime, maroon, navy, olive, orange, purple, red, silver, teal, white, and yellow. Browsers may recognize other keywords, such as the X11 color keywords that are documented in the W3C CSS3 Color module specification.

Number Values

A number value is expressed as a positive or negative number (when permitted). Numbers can be either real or integers, and some properties may restrict number values to integers. They may also restrict the range of acceptable values, as with color values that accept only integers in the range 0–255.

Percentage Values

A percentage value is expressed as a positive or negative number (when permitted), followed immediately by a percent sign (%). There should never be any space between the number and the percent sign. A percentage value will always be computed relative to something else. For example, declaring font-size: 120%; for an element sets the font size of that element at 120% the font-size of its parent element.

Length Values

A length value is expressed as a positive or negative number (when permitted), followed immediately by a two-letter abbreviation that represents the units to be used. There should never be any space between the number and the unit designator. Note that a value of 0 (zero) need not have a unit designator. Length units are divided into two types: *absolute units*, which are always measured in the same way, and *relative units*, which are measured in relation to other things.

Absolute length units

Inches (in)

As you might expect, the same inches found on typical U.S. rulers. The mapping from inches to a monitor or other display device is usually approximate at best, since many systems have no concept of the relation of their display areas to "real-world" measurements such as inches. Thus, inches should be used with extreme caution in screen design.

Centimeters (cm)

The centimeters found on rulers the world over. There are 2.54 cm to an inch, and one centimeter equals 0.394 inches. The same mapping warnings that applied to inches also apply to centimeters.

Millimeters (mm)

> There are 10 millimeters to a centimeter, so you get 25.4 mm to an inch, and 1 millimeter equals 0.0394 inches. Bear in mind the previous warnings about mapping lengths to monitors.

Points (pt)

> Points are standard typographical measures used by printers and typesetters for decades and by word-processing programs for many years. By modern definition, there are 72 points to an inch. Therefore, the capital letters of text set to 12 points should be a sixth of an inch tall. For example, P {font-size: 18pt;} is equivalent to P {font-size: 0.25in;}, assuming proper mapping of lengths to the display environment (see comments above).

Picas (pc)

> Another typographical term. A pica is equivalent to 12 points, which means there are 6 picas to an inch. The capital letters of text set to 1 pica should be a sixth of an inch tall. For example, P {font-size: 1.5pc;} would set text to be the same size as the example declarations found in the definition of points. Keep in mind previous warnings.

Relative length units

em-height (em)

> This refers to the em-height of a given font. In CSS, the em-height is equivalent to the height of the character box for a given font. Ems can be used to set relative sizes for fonts; for example, 1.2em is the same as saying 120%.

x-height (ex)

> This refers to the x-height of the font. However, the vast majority of fonts do not include their x-height, so many browsers approximate it (poorly) by simply setting 1ex to be equal to 0.5em. The exception is IE5/Mac, which

attempts to determine the actual x-height of a font by bit-mapping an "x" and counting pixels!

Pixels (px)

A pixel is a small box on screen, but CSS defines pixels more abstractly. In CSS terms, a pixel is defined to be about the size required to yield 96 pixels per inch. Most user agents ignore this definition in favor of simply addressing the pixels on the monitor. Scaling factors are brought into play when printing, although this scale cannot be relied upon.

URLs

url (<url>)

Used to point to a file such as a graphic. CSS defines URLs as relative to the stylesheet, but Netscape Navigator 4.x interprets URLs relative to the document being styled. Thanks to this bug, it is often recommended that absolute URLs be used instead of relative URLs.

Aural-Specific Values

The following values are used in conjunction with aural style properties in CSS2. These values were dropped from CSS2.1 due to a lack of support and are included here for the sake of completeness.

Angle values

Used to define the position from which a given sound should seem to originate. There are three type of angles: degrees (deg), grads (grad), and radians (rad). For example, a right angle could be declared as 90deg, 100grad, or 1.57rad; in each case, the values are translated into degrees in the range 0 through 360. This is also true of negative values, which are allowed. The measure -90deg is the same as 270deg.

Time values
> Used to specify delays between speaking elements; can be expressed as either milliseconds (ms) or seconds (s). Thus, 100ms and 0.1s are equivalent. Time values may not be negative, as CSS is supposed to avoid paradoxes.

Frequency values
> Used to declare frequencies for the sounds that speaking browsers can produce. Frequency values can be expressed as hertz (Hz) or megahertz (mHz) and cannot be negative. The value labels are case-insensitive, so 10mHz and 10mhz are equivalent.

Selectors

Universal Selector

Pattern:

```
*
```

Description:

This selector matches any element name in the document's language. If a rule does not have an explicit selector, then the universal selector is inferred.

Examples:

```
* {color: red;}
div * p {color: blue;}
```

Type Selector

Pattern:

```
element1
```

Description:

This selector matches the name of an element in the document's language. Every instance of the element name is matched. (CSS1 referred to these as "element selectors.")

Examples:

```
body {background: #FFF;}
p {font-size: 1em;}
```

Descendant Selector

Pattern:

```
element1 element2
```

Description:

This allows the author to select an element based on its status as a descendant of another element. The matched element can be a child, grandchild, great-grandchild, etc., of the ancestor element. (CSS1 referred to these as "contextual selectors.")

Examples:

```
body h1 {font-size: 200%;}
table tr td div ul li {color: purple;}
```

Child Selector

Pattern:

```
element1 > element2
```

Description:

This type of selector is used to match an element based on its status as a child of another element. This is more restrictive than a descendant selector, since only a child will be matched.

Examples:

```
div > p {color: cyan;}
ul > li {font-weight: bold;}
```

Adjacent Sibling Selector

Pattern:

```
element1 + element2
```

Description:

This allows the author to select an element that is the following adjacent sibling of another element. Any text between the two elements is ignored; only elements and their positions in the document tree are considered.

Examples:

```
table + p {margin-top: 2.5em;}
h1 + * {margin-top: 0;}
```

Class Selector

Pattern:

```
element1.classname
element1.classname1.classname2
```

Description:

In languages that permit it, such as HTML, XHTML, SVG, and MathML, a class selector using "dot notation" can be used to select elements that have a class containing a specific value or values. The name of the class value must immediately follow the dot. Multiple class values can be chained together. If no element name precedes the dot, then the selector matches all elements containing that class value or values.

Examples:

```
p.urgent {color: red;}
a.external {font-style: italic;}
.example {background: olive;}
.note.caution {background: yellow;}
```

ID Selector

Pattern:
```
element1#idname
```

Description:
In languages that permit it, such as HTML or XHTML, an ID selector using "hash notation" can be used to select elements that have an ID containing a specific value or values. The name of the ID value must immediately follow the octothorpe (#). If no element name precedes the octothorpe, then the selector matches all elements containing that ID value.

Examples:
```
h1#page-title {font-size: 250%;}
body#home {background: silver;}
#example {background: lime;}
```

Simple Attribute Selector

Pattern:
```
element1[attr]
```

Description:
This allows authors to select any element based on the presence of an attribute, regardless of the attribute's value.

Examples:
```
a[rel] {border-bottom: 3px double gray;}
p[class] {border: 1px dotted silver;}
```

Exact Attribute Value Selector

Pattern:
```
element1[attr="value"]
```

Description:

This allows authors to select any element based on the precise and complete value of an attribute.

Examples:
```
a[rel="Start"] {font-weight: bold;}
p[class="urgent"] {color: red;}
```

Partial Attribute Value Selector

Pattern:
```
element1[attr~="value"]
```

Description:

This allows authors to select any element based on a portion of the space-separated value of an attribute. Note that [class~="value"] is equivalent to .value (see above).

Examples:
```
a[rel~="friend"] {text-transform: uppercase;}
p[class~="warning"] {background: yellow;}
```

Language Attribute Selector

Pattern:
```
element1[lang|="lc"]
```

Description:

This allows authors to select any element with a lang attribute whose value is a hyphen-separated list of values, starting with the value provided in the selector.

Examples:
```
html[lang|="tr"] {color: red;}
```

Pseudo-Classes and Pseudo-Elements

:active

Type: Pseudo-class.

Applies to:

An element that is being activated.

Description:

This applies to an element during the period in which it is being activated. The most common example is clicking on a hyperlink in an HTML document: while the mouse button is being held down, the link is active. There are other ways to activate elements, and other elements can in theory be activated, although CSS doesn't define these.

Examples:

```
a:active {color: red;}
*:active {background: blue;}
```

:after

Type: Pseudo-element.

Generates:

A pseudo-element containing generated content placed after the content in the element.

Description:

This allows the author to insert generated content at the end of an element's content. By default, the pseudo-element is inline, but this can be changed using the property display.

Examples:

```
a.external:after {content: " " url(/icons/globe.gif);)
p:after {content: " | ";}
```

:before

Type: Pseudo-element.

Generates:

A pseudo-element containing generated content placed before the content in the element.

Description:

This allows the author to insert generated content at the beginning of an element's content. By default, the pseudo-element is inline, but this can be changed using the property display.

Examples:

```
a[href]:before {content: "[LINK] ";)
p:before {content: attr(class);}
a[rel~="met"]:after {content: " *";}
```

:first-child

Type: Pseudo-class.

Applies to:

Any element that is the first child of another element.

Description:

With this pseudo-class, an element is matched only when it is the first child of another element. For example, p:first-child will select any p element that is the first child of some other element. It does *not*, as is commonly assumed, select whatever element is the first child of a paragraph; for that, an author would write p > *: first-child.

Examples:

```
body *:first-child {font-weight: bold;}
p:first-child {font-size: 125%;}
```

:first-letter

Type: Pseudo-element.

Generates:
A pseudo-element that contains the first letter of an element.

Description:
This is used to style the first letter of an element. Any leading punctuation should be styled along with the first letter. Some languages have letter combinations that should be treated as a single character, and a user agent may apply the first letter style to both. Prior to CSS2.1, :first-letter could be attached only to block-level elements. CSS2.1 expands its scope to include block, list-item, table-call, table caption, and inline-block elements. There is a limited set of properties that can apply to a first letter.

Examples:
```
h1:first-letter {font-size: 166%;}
p:first-letter {text-decoration: underline;}
```

:first-line

Type: Pseudo-element.

Generates:
A pseudo-element that contains the first formatted line of an element.

Description:
This is used to style the first line of text in an element, no matter how many or few words may appear in that line.   :first-line can be attached only to block-level elements. There is a limited set of properties that can apply to a first line.

Examples:
```
p.lead:first-line {font-weight: bold;}
```

:focus

Type: Pseudo-class.

Applies to: An element that has focus.

Description:

This applies to an element during the period in which it has focus. One example from HTML is an input box that has the text-input cursor within it such that when the user starts typing, text will be entered into that box. Other elements, such as hyperlinks, can also have focus; however, CSS does not define which elements may have focus.

Examples:

```
a:focus {outline: 1px dotted red;}
input:focus {background: yellow;}
```

:hover

Type: Pseudo-class.

Applies to: An element that is in a hovered state.

Description:

This applies to an element during the period in which it is being *hovered* (when the user is designating an element without activating it). The most common example of this is moving the mouse pointer inside the boundaries of a hyperlink in an HTML document. Other elements can in theory be hovered, although CSS doesn't define which ones.

Examples:

```
a[href]:hover {text-decoration: underline;}
p:hover {background: yellow;}
```

:lang

Type: Pseudo-class.

Applies to: Any element with associated language-encoding information.

Description:

This matches elements based on their human-language encoding. Such language information must be contained within or otherwise associated with the document; it cannot be assigned from CSS. The handling of :lang is the same as for |= attribute selectors. For example, in an HTML document the language of an element is determined by its lang attribute. If the document does not have one, the language of an element is determined by the lang attribute of its nearest ancestor that does have one, and lacking that, by the Content-Language HTTP header response field (or the respective meta http-equiv) for the document.

Examples:

```
html:lang(en) {background: silver;}
*:lang(fr) {quotes: '« ' ' »';}
```

:link

Type: Pseudo-class.

Applies to: A hyperlink to another resource that has not been visited.

Description:

This applies to a link to a URI that has not been visited; that is, the URI to which the link points does not appear in the user agent's history. This state is mutually exclusive with the :visited state.

Examples:

```
a:link {color: blue;}
*:link {text-decoration: underline;}
```

:visited

Type: Pseudo-class.

Applies to: A hyperlink to another resource that has already been visited.

Description:

This applies to a link to a URI that has been visited; that is, the URI to which the link points appears in the user agent's history. This state is mutually exclusive with the :link state.

Examples:

```
a:visited {color: purple;}
*:visited {color: gray;}
```

Property Reference

Visual Media

background

Values:

[<background-color> || <background-image> || <background-repeat> || <background-attachment> || <background-position>] | inherit

Initial value: Refer to individual properties.

Applies to: All elements.

Inherited: No.

Percentages:

Values are allowed for <background-position>.

Computed value: See individual properties.

Description:

A shorthand way of expressing the various background properties using a single rule. Use of this property is encouraged over the other background properties because it is more widely supported and doesn't take as long to type. However, using it will set all of the allowed values (e.g., the repeat, position, and so on) to their defaults if the values are not explicitly declared. Thus the following two rules will have the same appearance:

```
background: yellow;
background: yellow none top left repeat;
```

Furthermore, these defaults can override previous declarations made with more specific background properties. For example, given the following rules:

```
H1 {background-repeat: repeat-x;}
H1, H2 {background: yellow url(headback.gif);}
```

the repeat value for both h1 and h2 elements will be set to the default of repeat, overriding the previously declared value of repeat-x.

Navigator 4.x is infamous for its inability to correctly render backgrounds. If there is no border around an element, then the background will only be visible behind the text of the element, instead of throughout the entire content area and padding. Unfortunately, if a border is added, there will be a transparent gap between the content area and the border itself. This is not the padding, and there is no way to get rid of the gap.

Examples:

```
BODY {background: white url(bg41.gif) fixed center repeat-
x;}
P {background: url(http://www.pix.org/stone.png) #555;}
PRE {background: yellow;}
```

background-attachment

Values:

scroll | fixed | inherit

Initial value:	scroll
Applies to:	All elements.
Inherited:	No.
Computed value:	As specified.

Description:

This property defines whether the background image scrolls along with the element when the document is scrolled. This property can be used to create "aligned" backgrounds; see *Chapter 9* of *Cascading Style Sheets: The Definitive Guide*, Second Edition (O'Reilly), for more details.

Examples:

```
body {background-attachment: scroll;}
div.fixbg {background-attachment: fixed;}
```

background-color

Values:

<color> | transparent | inherit

Initial value:	transparent
Applies to:	All elements.
Inherited:	No.
Computed value:	As specified.

Description:

This property sets a solid color for the background of the element. This color fills the content, padding, and border areas of the element, extending to the outer edge of the element's border. Borders that have transparent sections (such as dashed borders) will show the background color through the transparent sections.

Navigator 4.x insists on applying this value to the parent of an element, not the element itself. This can lead to "holes" in the parent element's background. Opera 4 has a bug that only shows up when a background has been repeated, and the rest of the background of the element is transparent (either by default or when explicitly declared). Scrolling the element "offscreen" and then bringing it back can cause "holes" to be punched through the repeated images of ancestor elements, thus creating visual anomalies.

Examples:

```
h4 {background-color: white;}
p {background-color: rgb(50%,50%,50%);}
pre {background-color: #FF9;}
```

background-image

Values:

<uri> | none | inherit

Initial value: none

Applies to: All elements.

Inherited: No.

Computed value: Absolute URI.

Description:

Places an image in the background of the element. Depending on the value of background-repeat, the image may tile infinitely, along one axis, or not at all. The initial background image (the origin image) is placed according to the value of background-position.

Examples:

```
body {background-image: url(bg41.gif);}
h2 {background-image: url(http://www.pix.org/dots.png);}
```

background-position

Values:

[[<percentage> | <length> | left | center | right] [<percentage> | <length> | top | center | bottom]?] | [[left | center | right] || [top | center | bottom]] | inherit

Initial value: 0%0%

Applies to: Block-level and replaced elements.

Inherited: No.

Percentages:

Refer to the corresponding point on both the element and the origin image.

Computed value:

The absolute length offsets if <length> is specified; otherwise, percentage values.

Description:

This property sets the position of the background's origin image (as defined by background-image); this is the point from which any background repetition or tiling will occur. Percentage values define not only a point within the element, but also the same point in the origin image itself, thus allowing (for example) an image to be centered by declaring its position to be 50% 50%. See Chapter 9 of *Cascading Style Sheets: The Definitive Guide*, Second Edition (O'Reilly), for more details.

When percentage or length values are used, the first is always the horizontal position, and the second the vertical. If only one value is given, it sets the horizontal position, while the missing value is assumed to be either center or 50%. Negative values are permitted, and may place the origin image outside the element's content area without actually rendering it.

Examples:

```
body {background-position: top center;}
div#navbar {background-position: right;}
pre {background-position: 10px 50%;}
```

background-repeat

Values:

repeat | repeat-x | repeat-y | no-repeat | inherit

Initial value: no-repeat

Applies to: All elements.

Inherited: No.

Computed value: As specified.

Description:

This property defines the tiling pattern for the background image.
Note that the axis-related repeat values actually cause repetition
in both directions along the relevant axis. The repetition begins
from the origin image, which is defined as the value of
background-image and is placed according to the value of
background-position.

Examples:

```
body {background-repeat: no-repeat;}
h2 {background-repeat: repeat-x;}
ul {background-repeat: repeat-y;}
```

border

Values:

[<border-width> || <border-style> || <border-color>] | inherit

Initial value: Refer to individual properties.

Applies to: All elements.

Inherited: No.

Computed value: As specified.

Description:

This is a shorthand property that defines the width, color, and
style of an element's border. Note that while none of the values
are actually required, omitting a border style will result in no
border being applied because the default border style is none. IE4
and IE5.0/Win do not apply borders to inline elements; IE5/Mac
and IE5.5+/Win do apply borders to inline elements.

Examples:

```
h1 {border: 2px dashed olive;}
a:link {border: blue solid 1px;}
p.warning {border: double 5px red;}
```

border-bottom

Values:

[<border-width> || <border-style> || <border-color>] | inherit

Initial value: Not defined for shorthand properties.

Applies to: All elements.

Inherited: No.

Computed value:

See individual properties (border-width, etc.).

Description:

This shorthand property defines the width, color, and style of the bottom border of an element. As with border, omission of a border style will result in no border appearing.

Examples:

```
ul {border-bottom: 0.5in groove green;}
a:active {border-bottom: purple 2px dashed;}
```

border-bottom-color

Values:

<color> | transparent | inherit

Initial value: The value of color for the element.

Applies to: All elements.

Inherited: No.

Computed value:

If no value is specified, use the computed value of the property color for the same element; otherwise, as specified.

Description:

This property sets the color for the visible portions of the bottom border of an element. Only a solid color can be defined, and the border's style must be something other than none or hidden for any visible border to appear.

Examples:

```
ul {border-bottom-color: green;}
a:active {border-bottom-color: purple;}
```

border-bottom-style

Values:

none | hidden | dotted | dashed | solid | double | groove | ridge | inset | outset | inherit

Initial value: none

Applies to: All elements.

Inherited: No.

Computed value: As specified.

Description:

This defines the style for the bottom border of an element. The value must be something other than none for any border to appear. In CSS1, HTML user agents were required to support only solid and none.

Examples:

```
ul {border-bottom-style: groove;}
a:active {border-bottom-style: dashed;}
```

border-bottom-width

Values:

thin | medium | thick | <length> | inherit

Initial value: medium

Applies to: All elements.

Inherited: No.

Computed value:

Absolute length; 0 if the style of the border is none or hidden.

Description:

This property sets the width for the bottom border of an element, which will take effect only if the border's style is something other than none. If the border style is none, then the border width is effectively reset to 0. Negative length values are not permitted.

Examples:

```
ul {border-bottom-width: 0.5in;}
a:active {border-bottom-width: 2px;}
```

border-color

Values:

[<color> | transparent]{1,4} | inherit

Initial value: Not defined for shorthand properties.

Applies to: All elements.

Inherited: No.

Computed value:

See individual properties (border-top-color, etc.).

Description:

This shorthand property sets the color for the visible portions of the overall border of an element or sets a different color for each of the four sides. Remember that a border's style must be something other than none or hidden for any visible border to appear.

Examples:

```
h1 {border-color: purple;}
a:visited {border-color: maroon;}
```

border-left

Values:
[<border-width> || <border-style> || <border-color>] | inherit

Initial value: Not defined for shorthand properties.

Applies to: All elements.

Inherited: No.

Computed value: See individual properties (border-width, etc.).

Description:
This shorthand property defines the width, color, and style of the left border of an element. As with border, omission of a border style will result in no border appearing.

Examples:
```
p {border-left: 3em solid gray;}
pre {border-left: double black 4px;}
```

border-left-color

Values:
<color> | transparent | inherit

Initial value: The value of color for the element.

Applies to: All elements.

Inherited: No.

Computed value:
If no value is specified, use the computed value of the property color for the same element; otherwise, as specified.

Description:
This property sets the color for the visible portions of the left border of an element. Only a solid color can be defined, and the

border's style must be something other than none or hidden for any visible border to appear.

Examples:

```
p {border-left-color: gray;}
pre {border-left-color: black;}
```

border-left-style

Values:

none | hidden | dotted | dashed | solid | double | groove | ridge | inset | outset | inherit

Initial value:	none
Applies to:	All elements.
Inherited:	No.
Computed value:	As specified.

Description:

This defines the style for the left border of an element. The value must be something other than none for any border to appear. In CSS1, HTML user agents were required to support only solid and none.

Examples:

```
p {border-left-style: solid;}
pre {border-left-style: double;}
```

border-left-width

Values:

thin | medium | thick | <length> | inherit

Initial value:	medium
Applies to:	All elements.
Inherited:	No.

Computed value:

Absolute length; 0 if the style of the border is none or hidden.

Description:

This sets the width for the left border of an element, which will take effect only if the border's style is something other than none. If the border style is none, then the border width is effectively reset to 0. Negative length values are not permitted.

Examples:

```
p {border-left-width: 3em;}
pre {border-left-width: 4px;}
```

border-right

Values:

[<border-width> || <border-style> || <border-color>] | inherit

Initial value:	Not defined for shorthand properties.
Applies to:	All elements.
Inherited:	No.
Computed value:	See individual properties (border-width, etc.).

Description:

This shorthand property defines the width, color, and style of the right border of an element. As with border, omission of a border style will result in no border appearing.

Examples:

```
img {border-right: 30px dotted blue;}
h3 {border-right: cyan 1em inset;}
```

border-right-color

Values:

<color> | transparent | inherit

Initial value:	The value of color for the element.
Applies to:	All elements.
Inherited:	No.

Computed value:

If no value is specified, use the computed value of the property color for the same element; otherwise, as specified.

Description:

This property sets the color for the visible portions of the right border of an element. Only a solid color can be defined, and the border's style must be something other than none or hidden for any visible border to appear.

Examples:

```
img {border-right-color: blue;}
h3 {border-right-color: cyan;}
```

border-right-style

Values:

none | hidden | dotted | dashed | solid | double | groove | ridge | inset | outset | inherit

Initial value:	none
Applies to:	All elements.
Inherited:	No.
Computed value:	As specified.

Description:

This defines the style for the right border of an element. The value must be something other than none for any border to appear. In CSS1, HTML user agents were required to support only solid and none.

Examples:

```
img {border-right-style: dotted;}
h3 {border-right-style: inset;}
```

border-right-width

Values:

thin | medium | thick | <length> | inherit

Initial value: medium

Applies to: All elements.

Inherited: No.

Computed value:

Absolute length; 0 if the style of the border is none or hidden.

Description:

This sets the width for the right border of an element, which will take effect only if the border's style is something other than none. If the border style is none, then the border width is effectively reset to 0. Negative length values are not permitted.

Examples:

```
img {border-right-width: 30px;}
h3 {border-right-width: 1em;}
```

border-style

Values:

[none | hidden | dotted | dashed | solid | double | groove | ridge | inset | outset]{1,4} | inherit

Initial value: Not defined for shorthand properties.

Applies to: All elements.

Inherited: No.

Computed value:

See individual properties (border-top-style, etc.).

Description:

This shorthand property can be used to set the styles for the overall border of an element or for each side individually. The value of any border must be something other than none for the border to appear.

Note that setting border-style to none (its default value) will result in no border at all. In such a case, any value of border-width will be ignored and the width of the border set to 0. CCS1 requires HTML users agents to support only solid and none. Any unrecognized value from the list of values should be reinterpreted as solid.

Navigator 4.x does not reset the border-width to 0 if border-style is none, but instead incorrectly honors the width setting.

Examples:

```
h1 {border-style: solid;}
img {border-style: inset;}
```

border-top

Values:

[<border-width> || <border-style> || <border-color>] | inherit

Initial value: Not defined for shorthand properties.

Applies to: All elements.

Inherited: No.

Computed value: See individual properties (border-width, etc.).

Description:

This shorthand property defines the width, color, and style of the top border of an element. As with border, omission of a border style will result in no border appearing.

Examples:

```
ul {border-top: 0.5in solid black;}
h1 {border-top: dashed 1px gray;}
```

border-top-color

Values:

<color> | transparent | inherit

Initial value: The value of color for the element.

Applies to: All elements.

Inherited: No.

Computed value:

If no value is specified, use the computed value of the property color for the same element; otherwise, as specified.

Description:

This property sets the color for the visible portions of the top border of an element. Only a solid color can be defined, and the border's style must be something other than none or hidden for any visible border to appear.

Examples:

```
ul {border-top-color: black;}
h1 {border-top-color: gray;}
```

border-top-style

Values:

none | hidden | dotted | dashed | solid | double | groove | ridge | inset | outset | inherit

Initial value: none

Applies to: All elements.

| **Inherited:** | No. |
| **Computed value:** | As specified. |

Description:

This defines the style for the top border of an element. The value must be something other than none for any border to appear. In CSS1, HTML user agents were required to support only solid and none.

Examples:

```
ul {border-top-style: solid;}
h1 {border-top-style: dashed;}
```

border-top-width

Values:

thin | medium | thick | <length> | inherit

Initial value:	medium
Applies to:	All elements.
Inherited:	No.

Computed value:

Absolute length; 0 if the style of the border is none or hidden.

Description:

This sets the width for the top border of an element, which will take effect only if the border's style is something other than none. If the style is none, then the width is effectively reset to 0. Negative length values are not permitted.

Examples:

```
ul {border-top-width: 0.5in;}
h1 {border-top-width: 1px;}
```

border-width

Values:
[thin | medium | thick | <length>]{1,4} | inherit

Initial value: Not defined for shorthand properties.

Applies to: All elements.

Inherited: No.

Computed value:
See individual properties (border-top-style, etc.).

Description:
This shorthand property can be used to set the width for the overall border of an element or for each side individually. The width will take effect for a given border only if the border's style is something other than none. If the border style is none, then the border width is effectively reset to 0. Negative length values are not permitted.

Examples:
```
h1 {border-width: 2ex;}
img {border-width: 5px;}
```

bottom

Values:
<length> | <percentage> | auto | inherit

Initial value: auto

Applies to:
Positioned elements (that is, elements for which the value of position is something other than static).

Inherited: No.

Percentages: Refer to the height of the containing block.

Computed value:

For relatively positioned elements, see note; for static elements, auto; for length values, the corresponding absolute length; for percentage values, the specified value; otherwise, auto.

Note:

For relatively positioned elements, if both bottom and top are auto, their computed values are both 0; if one of them is auto, it becomes the negative of the other; if neither is auto, bottom will become the negative of the value of top.

Description:

This property defines the offset between the bottom outer margin edge of a positioned element and the bottom edge of its containing block.

Examples:

```
div#footer {position: fixed; bottom: 0;}
sup {position: relative; bottom: 0.5em; vertical-align:
baseline;}
```

clear

Values:

left | right | both | none

Initial value: none

Applies to: Block-level elements.

Inherited: No.

Computed value: As specified.

Description:

This defines the sides of an element on which no floating elements may appear. In CSS1 and CSS2, this is accomplished by automatically increasing the top margin of the cleared element. In CSS2.1, clearance space is added above the element's top margin, but the margin itself is not altered. In either case, the end result is that the element's top outer border edge is just below the bottom outer margin edge of a floated element on the declared side.

Examples:

```
h1 {clear: both;}
h3 {clear: right;}
```

clip

Values:

rect(*top*, *right*, *bottom*, *left*) | auto | inherit

Initial value: auto

Applies to:

Absolutely positioned elements (in CSS2, clip applied to block-level and replaced elements).

Inherited: No.

Computed value:

For a rectangle, a set of four computed lengths representing the edges of the clipping rectangle; otherwise, as specified.

Description:

This is used to define a clipping rectangle inside of which the content of an absolutely positioned element is visible. Content outside this clipping area is treated according to the value of overflow. The clipping area can be smaller or larger than the content area of the element.

Examples:

```
div.sidebar {overflow: scroll; clip: 0 0 5em 10em;}
img.tiny {overflow: hidden; clip: 5px 5px 20px 20px;}
```

color

Values:

<color> | inherit

Initial value:	User agent–specific.
Applies to:	All elements.
Inherited:	Yes.
Computed value:	As specified.

Description:

This property sets the foreground color of an element, which in HTML rendering means the text of an element; raster images are not affected by color. This is also the color applied to any borders of the element, unless overridden by border-color or one of the other border color properties (border-top-color, etc.).

Examples:

```
strong {color: rgb(255,128,128);}
h3 {color: navy;}
p.warning {color: #ff0000;}
pre.pastoral {color: #0f0;}
```

content

Values:

normal | [<string> | <uri> | <counter> | attr(<identifier>)| open-quote | close-quote | no-open-quote | no-close-quote]+ | inherit

Initial value:	normal
Applies to:	:before and :after pseudo-elements.
Inherited:	No.

Computed value:

For <uri> values, an absolute URI; for attribute references, the resulting string; otherwise, as specified.

Description:

This is the property used to define the generated content placed before or after an element. By default, this is likely to be inline content, but the type of box the content creates can be controlled using the property display.

Examples:

```
p:before {content: "Paragraph...";}
img:after {content: attr(src);}
a[href]:after {content: "(" attr(href) ")"; font-size:
smaller;}
```

---

counter-increment

Values:

[<identifier> <integer>?]+ | none | inherit

Initial value: User agent–dependent.

Applies to: All elements.

Inherited: No.

Computed value: As specified.

Description:

With this property, counters can be incremented (or decremented) by any value, positive or negative. If no <integer> is supplied, it defaults to 1.

Examples:

```
h1 {counter-increment: section;}
*.backward li {counter-increment: counter -1;}
```

---

counter-reset

Values:

[<identifier> <integer>?]+ | none | inherit

Initial value: User agent-dependent.

Applies to: All elements.

Inherited: No.

Computed value: As specified.

Description:

With this property, counters can be reset (or set for the first time) to any value, positive or negative. If no <integer> is supplied, it defaults to 0.

Examples:

```
h1 {counter-reset: section;}
h2 {counter-reset: subsec 1;}
```

---

cursor

Values:

[[<uri>,]* [auto | default | pointer | crosshair | move | e-resize | ne-resize | nw-resize | n-resize | se-resize | sw-resize | s-resize | w-resize| text | wait | help | progress]] | inherit

Initial value: auto

Applies to: All elements.

Inherited: Yes.

Computed value:

For <uri> values, an absolute URI; otherwise, as specified.

Description:

This defines the cursor shape to be used when a mouse pointer is placed within the boundary of an element (although CSS2.1 does not define which edge creates this boundary). Authors are cautioned to remember that users are typically very aware of cursor changes, and can be easily confused by changes that seem counterintuitive. For example, making any noninteractive element switch the cursor state to pointer is quite likely to cause user frustration.

<uri> values are supported only by IE6/Win as of this writing.

Examples:

```
a.moreinfo {cursor: help;}
a[href].external {cursor: url(globe.ani);}
```

direction

Values:

ltr | rtl | inherit

Initial value:	ltr
Applies to:	All elements.
Inherited:	Yes.
Computed value:	As specified.

Description:

This property specifies the base writing direction of blocks and the direction of embeddings and overrides for the Unicode bidirectional algorithm. User agents that do not support bidirectional text are permitted to ignore this property.

Examples:

```
*:lang(en) {direction: ltr;}
*:lang(ar) {direction: rtl;}
```

display

Values:

none | inline | block | inline-block | list-item | run-in | table | inline-table | table-row-group | table-header-group | table-footer-group | table-row | table-column-group | table-column | table-cell | table-caption | inherit

Initial value:	inline
Applies to:	All elements.
Inherited:	No.

Computed value:

Varies for floated, positioned, and root elements (see CSS2.1, section 9.7); otherwise, as specified.

Note:

The values `compact` and `marker` appeared in CSS2 but were dropped from CSS2.1 due to a lack of widespread support.

Description:

This is used to define the kind of display box an element generates during layout. Gratuitous use of `display` with a document type such as HTML can be dangerous, as it upsets the display hierarchy already defined in HTML. In the case of XML, which has no such built-in hierarchy, `display` is indispensable.

Examples:

```
h1 {display: block;}
li {display: list-item;}
img {display: inline;}
.hide {display: none;}
tr {table-row;}
```

float

Values:

left | right | none | inherit

Initial value: none

Applies to: All elements.

Inherited: No.

Computed value: As specified.

Description:

`float` defines the direction in which an element is floated. This has traditionally been applied to images in order to let text flow around them, but in CSS, any element may be floated. A floated element will generate a block-level box no matter what kind of element it may be. Floated nonreplaced elements should be given an explicit width, as they otherwise tend to become as narrow as possible. Basic floating is generally supported by all browsers, especially on images, but the nature of floats can lead to unexpected results when they are used as a page layout mechanism. Use float cautiously and thoroughly test any pages employing it.

Examples:

```
img.figure {float: left;}
p.sidebar {float: right; width: 15em;}
```

font

Values:

[[<font-style> || <font-variant> || <font-weight>]? <font-size> [/ <line-height>]? <font-family>] | caption | icon | menu | message-box | small-caption | status-bar | inherit

Initial value: Refer to individual properties.

Applies to: All elements.

Inherited: Yes.

Percentages:

Calculated with respect to the parent element for <font-size> and with respect to the element's <font-size> for <line-height>.

Computed value: See individual properties (font-style, etc.).

Description:

This is a shorthand property used to set two or more aspects of an element's font all at once. It can also be used to set the element's font to match an aspect of the user's computing environment using keywords such as icon. Note that if these keywords are not used, the minimum font value must include the font size and family in that order.

Examples:

```
p {font: small-caps italic bold small/1.25em
Helvetica,sans-serif;}
p.example {font: 14px Arial;} /* technically correct,
although
     generic font-families are encouraged for fallback
purposes */
.figure span {font: icon;}
```

font-family

Values:

[[<family-name> | <generic-family>],]*   [<family-name> |
<generic-family>] | inherit

Initial value:	User agent-specific.
Applies to:	All elements.
Inherited:	Yes.
Computed value:	As specified.

Description:

This defines a font family to be used in the display of an element's text. Note that use of a specific font family (e.g., Geneva) is wholly dependent on that family being available on a user's machine; no font downloading is implied by this property. Therefore, the use of generic family names as a fallback is strongly encouraged. Font names that contain spaces or nonalphabetic characters should be quoted in order to minimize potential confusion.

Examples:

```
p {font-family: Helvetica, Arial, sans-serif;}
li {font-family: Times, TimesNR, "New Century Schoolbook",
serif;}
pre {font-family: Courier, "Courier New", "Andale Mono",
Monaco, monospace;}
```

font-size

Values:

xx-small | x-small | small | medium | large | x-large | xx-large | smaller | larger | <length> | <percentage> | inherit

Initial value:	medium
Applies to:	All elements.
Inherited:	Yes.

Percentages:

Calculated with respect to the parent element's font size.

Computed value: An absolute length.

Description:

This property sets the size of the font. The size can be defined as an absolute size, a relative size, a length value, or a percentage value. Negative length and percentage values are not permitted.

The dangers of font-size assignment are many and varied, and points are particularly discouraged in web design, as there is no certain relationship between points and the pixels on a monitor. Note also that, due to early misunderstandings, setting the font-size to medium will lead to different results in Internet Explorer and Navigator 4.x. Some of these problems are covered in Chapter 5 of *Cascading Style Sheets: The Definitive Guide*, Second Edition (O'Reilly); for further discussion, refer to *http://style.cleverchimp.com/*.

For best results, authors are encouraged to use either percentages or em units for font sizing. As a last resort, pixel sizes can be used, but this approach has serious accessibility penalties since it prevents users from resizing text in IE/Win, even if it is too small to read comfortably. Most other browsers allow the user to resize text no matter how it has been sized.

Examples:

```
h2 {font-size: 200%;}
code {font-size: 0.9em;}
p.caption {font-size: 9px;}
```

font-style

Values:

italic | oblique | normal | inherit

Initial value: normal

Applies to: All elements.

Inherited: Yes.

Computed value: As specified.

Description:

This sets the font to use an italic, oblique, or normal font face. Italic text is generally defined as a separate face within the font family. It is theoretically possible for a user agent to compute a slanted font face from the normal face. However, the reality is that user agents rarely recognize the difference between italic and oblique text, and almost always render both in exactly the same way.

Examples:

```
em {font-style: oblique;}
i {font-style: italic;}
```

font-variant

Values:

small-caps | normal | inherit

Initial value: normal

Applies to: All elements.

Inherited: Yes.

Computed value: As specified.

Description:

This property is basically used to define small-caps text. It is theoretically possible for a user agent to compute a small-caps font face from the normal face.

Examples:

```
h3 {font-variant: small-caps;}
p {font-variant: normal;}
```

font-weight

Values:

normal | bold | bolder | lighter | 100 | 200 | 300 | 400 | 500| 600 |
700 | 800 | 900 | inherit

Initial value: normal

Applies to: All elements.

Inherited: Yes.

Computed value:

One of the numeric values (100, etc.), or one of the numeric values plus one of the relative values (bolder or lighter).

Description:

This property sets the font weight used in rendering an element's text. The numeric value 400 is equivalent to the keyword normal, and 700 is equivalent to bold. Each numeric value must be at least as light as the next lowest number and at least as heavy as the next highest number. Thus, if a font has only two weights—normal and bold—then the numbers 100 through 500 will be normal, and 600 through 900 will be bold.

Examples:

```
b {font-weight: 700;}
strong {font-weight: bold;}
.delicate {font-weight: lighter;}
```

height

Values:

<length> | <percentage> | auto | inherit

Initial value: auto

Applies to: Block-level and replaced elements.

Inherited: No.

Percentages: Calculated with respect to the height of the containing block.

Computed value:

For auto and percentage values, as specified; otherwise, an absolute length, unless the property does not apply to the element (then auto).

Description:

This defines the height of an element's content area, outside of which padding, borders, and margins are added. This property is ignored for inline nonreplaced elements. Negative length and percentage values are not permitted.

Examples:

```
img.icon {height: 50px;}
h1 {height: 1.75em;}
```

left

Values:

<length> | <percentage> | auto | inherit

Initial value: auto

Applies to: Positioned elements (that is, elements for which the value of position is something other than static).

| **Inherited:** | No. |
| **Percentages:** | Refer to the width of the containing block. |

Computed value:

For relatively positioned elements, see note; for static elements, auto; for length values, the corresponding absolute length; for percentage values, the specified value; otherwise, auto.

Note:

For relatively positioned elements, the computed value of left always equals -right.

Description:

This property defines the offset between the left outer margin edge of a positioned element and the left edge of its containing block.

Examples:

```
div#footer {position: fixed; left: 0;}
*.hanger {position: relative; left: -25px;}
```

---

letter-spacing

Values:

<length> | normal | inherit

Initial value:	normal
Applies to:	All elements.
Inherited:	Yes.
Computed value:	For length values, the absolute length; otherwise, normal.

Description:

This defines the amount of whitespace to be inserted between the character boxes of text. Since character glyphs are typically narrower than their character boxes, length values create a modifier to the usual spacing between letters. Thus, normal is

---

synonymous with 0. Negative length values are permitted and will cause letters to bunch closer together.

Examples:

```
p.spacious {letter-spacing: 6px;}
em {letter-spacing: 0.2em;}
p.cramped {letter-spacing: -0.5em;}
```

line-height

Values:

<length> | <percentage> | <number> | normal | inherit

Initial value:	normal
Applies to:	All elements (but see text regarding replaced and block-level elements).
Inherited:	Yes.
Percentages:	Relative to the font size of the element.
Computed value:	For length and percentage values, the absolute value; otherwise, as specified.

Description:

This property influences the layout of line boxes. When applied to a block-level element, it defines the minimum distance between baselines within that element, but not the maximum. The difference between the computed values of line-height and font-size (called "leading" in CSS) is split in half and added to the top and bottom of each piece of content in a line of text. The shortest box that can enclose all those pieces of content is the line box. A raw number value assigns a scaling factor, which is inherited instead of a computed value. Negative values are not permitted. (Navigator 4.x incorrectly permits negative values for this property.)

Examples:

```
p {line-height: 1.5em;}
h2 {line-height: 200%;}
ul {line-height: 1.2;}
pre {line-height: 0.75em;}
```

list-style

Values:

[<list-style-type> || <list-style-image> || <list-style-position>] | inherit

Initial value: Refer to individual properties.

Applies to: Elements whose display value is list-item.

Inherited: Yes.

Computed value: See individual properties.

Description:

This is a shorthand property that condenses all the other list-style properties. Because it applies to any element that has a display of list-item, it will apply only to li elements in ordinary HTML and XHTML, although it can be applied to any element and inherited by list-item elements.

Examples:

```
ul {list-style: square url(bullet3.gif) outer;} /* values
are inherited by 'li' elements */
ol {list-style: upper-roman;}
```

list-style-image

Values:

<uri> | none | inherit

Initial value: none

Applies to: Elements whose display value is list-item.

Inherited: Yes.

Computed value: For <uri> values, the absolute URI; otherwise, none.

Description:

This specifies an image to be used as the marker on an ordered or unordered list item. The placement of the image with respect to the content of the list item can be broadly controlled using list-style-position.

Examples:

```
ul {list-style-image: url(bullet3.gif);}
ul li {list-style-image: url(http://example.org/pix/
checkmark.png);}
```

list-style-position

Values:

inside | outside | inherit

Initial value: outside

Applies to: Elements whose display value is list-item.

Inherited: Yes.

Computed value: As specified.

Description:

This property is used to declare the position of the list marker with respect to the content of the list item. Outside markers are placed some distance from the border edge of the list item, but the distance is not defined in CSS. Inside markers are treated as though they were an inline element inserted at the beginning of the list item's content.

Examples:

```
li {list-style-position: outside;}
ol li {list-style-position: inside;}
```

list-style-type

CSS2.1 values:

```
disc | circle | square | decimal | decimal-leading-zero |
lower-roman | upper-roman | lower-greek | lower-latin |
armenian | georegian | none | inherit
```

CSS2 values:

```
disc | circle | square | decimal | decimal-leading-zero | upper-
alpha | lower-alpha | upper-roman | lower-roman | lower-greek|
hebrew | armenian | georgian | cjk-ideographic | hiragana |
katakana | hiragana-iroha | none | inherit
```

Initial value: disc

Applies to: Elements whose display value is list-item.

Inherited: Yes.

Computed value: As specified.

Description:

This is used to declare the type of marker system to be used in the presentation of a list. There is no defined behavior for what happens when a list using an alphabetic ordering exceeds the letters in the list. For example, once an upper-latin list reaches "Z", the specification does not say what the next bullet should be. (Two possible answers are "AA" and "ZA".)

Examples:

```
ul {list-style-type: square;}
ol {list-style-type: lower-roman;}
```

margin

Values:

[<length> | <percentage> | auto]{1,4} | inherit

Initial value: Not defined.

Applies to:	All elements.
Inherited:	No.
Percentages:	Refer to the width of the containing block.
Computed value:	See individual properties.

Description:

This shorthand property sets the width of the overall margin for an element or sets the widths of each individual side margin. Vertically adjacent margins of block-level elements are collapsed, whereas inline elements effectively do not take top and bottom margins. The left and right margins of inline elements do not collapse, nor do margins on floated elements. Negative margin values are permitted, but caution is warranted, because negative values can cause elements to overwrite other parts of a page or to appear to be wider than their parent elements.

Examples:

```
h1 {margin: 2ex;}
p {margin: auto;}
img {margin: 10px;}
```

margin-bottom

Values:

<length> | <percentage> | auto | inherit

Initial value:	0
Applies to:	All elements.
Inherited:	No.
Percentages:	Refer to the width of the containing block.
Computed value:	For percentages, as specified; for length values, the absolute length.

Description:

This sets the width of the bottom margin for an element. Negative values are permitted, but caution is warranted.

Examples:

```
ul {margin-bottom: 0.5in;}
h1 {margin-bottom: 2%;}
```

margin-left

Values:

<length> | <percentage> | auto | inherit

Initial value:	0
Applies to:	All elements.
Inherited:	No.
Percentages:	Refer to the width of the containing block.
Computed value:	For percentages, as specified; for length values, the absolute length.

Description:

This sets the width of the left margin for an element. Negative values are permitted, but caution is warranted.

Examples:

```
p {margin-left: 5%;}
pre {margin-left: 3em;}
```

margin-right

Values:

<length> | <percentage> | auto | inherit

Initial value:	0
Applies to:	All elements.

Inherited:	No.
Percentages:	Refer to the width of the containing block.
Computed value:	For percentages, as specified; for length values, the absolute length.

Description:

This sets the width of the right margin for an element. Negative values are permitted, but caution is warranted.

Examples:

```
img {margin-right: 30px;}
ol {margin-right: 5em;}
```

margin-top

Values:

<length> | <percentage> | auto | inherit

Initial value:	0
Applies to:	All elements.
Inherited:	No.
Percentages:	Refer to the width of the containing block.
Computed value:	For percentages, as specified; for length values, the absolute length.

Description:

This sets the width of the top margin for an element. Negative values are permitted, but caution is warranted.

Examples:

```
ul {margin-top: 0.5in;}
h3 {margin-top: 1.5em;}
```

max-height

Values:

<length> | <percentage> | none | inherit

Initial value: none

Applies to: All elements except inline nonreplaced elements and table elements.

Inherited: No.

Percentages: Refer to the height of the containing block.

Computed value: For percentages, as specified; for length values, the absolute length; otherwise, none.

Description:

The value of this property sets a maximum constraint on the height of the element. Thus, the element can be shorter than the specified value, but not taller. Negative values are not permitted.

Examples:

```
div#footer {max-height: 3em;}
```

max-width

Values:

<length> | <percentage> | none | inherit

Initial value: none

Applies to: All elements except inline nonreplaced elements and table elements.

Inherited: No.

Percentages: Refer to the height of the containing block.

Computed value: For percentages, as specified; for length values, the absolute length; otherwise, none.

Description:

The value of this property sets a maximum constraint on the width of the element. Thus, the element can be narrower than the specified value, but not wider. Negative values are not permitted.

Examples:

```
#sidebar img {width: 50px; max-width: 100%;}
```

---

min-height

Values:

<length> | <percentage> | inherit

Initial value:	0
Applies to:	All elements except inline nonreplaced elements and table elements.
Inherited:	No.
Percentages:	Refer to the width of the containing block.
Computed value:	For percentages, as specified; for length values, the absolute length.

Description:

The value of this property sets a minimum constraint on the height of the element. Thus, the element can be taller than the specified value, but not shorter. Negative values are not permitted.

Examples:

```
div#footer {min-height: 1em;}
```

---

min-width

Values:

<length> | <percentage> | inherit

Initial value:	0
Applies to:	All elements except inline nonreplaced elements and table elements.
Inherited:	No.
Percentages:	Refer to the width of the containing block.
Computed value:	For percentages, as specified; for length values, the absolute length; otherwise, none.

Description:

The value of this property sets a minimum constraint on the width of the element. Thus, the element can be wider than the specified value, but not narrower. Negative values are not permitted.

Examples:

```
div.aside {float: right; width: 13em; max-width: 33%;}
```

---

outline

Values:

[<outline-color> || <outline-style> || <outline-width>] | inherit

Initial value:	Not defined for shorthand properties.
Applies to:	All elements.
Inherited:	No.
Computed value:	See individual properties (outline-color, etc.).

Description:

This shorthand property is used to set the overall outline for an element. Outlines can be of irregular shape, and they do not change or otherwise affect the placement of elements.

Examples:

```
*[href]:focurs {outline: 2px dashed invert;}
form:focus {outline: outset cyan 0.25em;}
```

---

outline-color

Values:

<color> | invert | inherit

Initial value: invert (see Description, below)

Applies to: All elements.

Inherited: No.

Computed value: As specified.

Description:

This property sets the color for the visible portions of the overall outline of an element. Remember that an outline's style must be something other than none for any visible border to appear. User agents are permitted to ignore invert on platforms that don't support color inversion. In that case, the default is the value of color for the element.

Examples:

```
*[href]:focurs {outline-color: invert;}
form:focus {outline-color: cyan;}
```

outline-style

Values:

none | dotted | dashed | solid | double | groove | ridge | inset | outset | inherit

Initial value: none

Applies to: All elements

Inherited: No.

Computed value: As specified.

Description:

This property is used to set the style for the overall border of an element. The style must be something other than none for any outline to appear.

Examples:

```
*[href]:focus {outline-style: dashed;}
form:focus {outline-style: outset;}
```

outline-width

Values:

thin | medium | thick | <length> | inherit

Initial value:	medium
Applies to:	All elements.
Inherited:	No.
Computed value:	Absolute length; 0 if the style of the border is none or hidden.

Description:

This property sets the width for the overall outline of an element. The width will take effect only for a given outline if the outline's style is something other than none. If the style is none, then the width is effectively reset to 0. Negative length values are not permitted.

Examples:

```
*[href]:focus {outline-width: 2px;}
form:focus {outline-width: 0.25em;}
```

overflow

Values:

visible | hidden | scroll | auto | inherit

Initial value:	visible
Applies to:	Block-level and replaced elements.
Inherited:	No.
Computed value:	As specified.

Description:

This defines what happens to content that overflows the content area of an element. For the value `scroll`, user agents should provide a scrolling mechanism whether or not it is actually needed; thus, for example, scrollbars would appear even if all content is able to fit within the element box.

Examples:

```
#masthead {overflow: hidden;}
object {overflow: scroll;}
```

padding

Values:
[<length> | <percentage>]{1,4} | `inherit`

Initial value:	Not defined for shorthand elements.
Applies to:	All elements.
Inherited:	No.
Percentages:	Refer to the width of the containing block.
Computed value:	See individual properties (`padding-top`, etc.).
Note:	Padding can never be negative.

Description:

This shorthand property sets the width of the overall padding for an element or sets the widths of each individual side padding. Padding set on inline nonreplaced elements does not affect line-height calculations; therefore, such an element with both padding and a background may visibly extend into other lines and potentially overlap other content. The background of the element will extend throughout the padding. Negative padding values are not permitted.

Examples:

```
h1 {padding: 2ex;}
img {padding: 10px;}
```

padding-bottom

Values:

<length> | <percentage> | inherit

Initial value:	0
Applies to:	All elements.
Inherited:	No.
Percentages:	Refer to the width of the containing block.
Computed value:	For percentage values, as specified; for length values, the absolute length.

Note:

Padding can never be negative.

Description:

This property sets the width of the bottom padding for an element. Bottom padding set on inline nonreplaced elements does not affect line-height calculations; therefore, such an element with both bottom padding and a background may visibly extend into other lines and potentially overlap other content. Negative padding values are not permitted.

Examples:

```
ul {padding-bottom: 0.5in;}
h1 {padding-bottom: 2%;}
```

padding-left

Values:

<length> | <percentage> | inherit

Initial value:	0
Applies to:	All elements.
Inherited:	No.
Percentages:	Refer to the width of the containing block.
Computed value:	For percentage values, as specified; for length values, the absolute length.
Note:	Padding can never be negative.

Description:

This property sets the width of the left padding for an element. Left padding set for an inline nonreplaced element will appear only on the left edge of the first inline box generated by the element. Negative padding values are not permitted.

Examples:

```
p {padding-left: 5%;}
pre {padding-left: 3em;}
```

---

padding-right

Values:

<length> | <percentage> | inherit

Initial value:	0
Applies to:	All elements.
Inherited:	No.
Percentages:	Refer to the width of the containing block.

| **Computed value:** | For percentage values, as specified; for length values, the absolute length. |

Note:

Padding can never be negative.

Description:

This property sets the width of the right padding for an element. Right padding set for an inline nonreplaced element will appear only on the right edge of the last inline box generated by the element. Negative padding values are not permitted.

Examples:

```
img {padding-right: 30px;}
ol {padding-right: 5em;}
```

---

padding-top

Values:

<length> | <percentage> | inherit

Initial value:	0
Applies to:	All elements.
Inherited:	No.
Percentages:	Refer to the width of the containing block.
Computed value:	For percentage values, as specified; for length values, the absolute length.

Note:

Padding can never be negative.

Description:

This property sets the width of the top padding for an element. Top padding set on inline nonreplaced elements does not affect line-height calculations; therefore, such an element with both top padding and a background may visibly extend into other lines and

---

potentially overlap other content. Negative padding values are not permitted.

Examples:
```
ul {padding-top: 0.5in;}
h3 {padding-top: 1.5em;}
```

position

Values:

static | relative | absolute | fixed | inherit

Initial value: static

Applies to: All elements.

Inherited: No.

Computed value: As specified.

Description:

This defines the positioning scheme used to lay out an element. Any element may be positioned, although elements positioned with absolute or fixed will generate a block-level box no matter what kind of element it is. An element that is relatively positioned is offset from its default placement in the normal flow.

Examples:
```
#footer {position: fixed; bottom: 0;}
*.offset {position: relative; top: 0.5em;}
```

quotes

Values:

[<string> <string>]+ | none | inherit

Initial value: User agent–dependent.

Applies to: All elements.

Inherited: Yes.

Computed value: As specified.

Description:

This property is used to determine the quotation pattern used with quotes and nested quotes. The actual quote marks are inserted via the property content.

Examples:

    q {quotes: '\201C' '\201D' '\2018' '\2019';}

---

right

Values:

<length> | <percentage> | auto | inherit

Initial value: auto

Applies to: Positioned elements (that is, elements for which the value of position is something other than static).

Inherited: No.

Percentages: Refer to the width of the containing block.

Computed value:

For relatively positioned elements, see the following note; for static elements, auto; for length values, the corresponding absolute length; for percentage values, the specified value; otherwise, auto.

Note:

For relatively positioned elements, the computed value of left always equals right.

Description:

This property defines the offset between the right outer margin edge of a positioned element and the right edge of its containing block.

Examples:

```
div#footer {position: fixed; right: 0;}
*.overlapper {position: relative; right: -25px;}
```

text-align

CSS2.1values:

left | center | right | justify | inherit

CSS2 values:

left | center | right | justify | <string> | inherit

Initial value:	User agent–specific; may also depend on writing direction.
Applies to:	Block-level elements.
Inherited:	Yes.
Computed value:	As specified.

Note:

CSS2 included a <string> value that was dropped from CSS2.1 due to a lack of support.

Description:

This property sets the horizontal alignment of text within a block-level element by defining the point to which line boxes are aligned. The value justify is supported by allowing user agents to programmatically adjust the letter and word spacing of the line's content; results may vary by user agent.

Examples:

```
p {text-align: justify;}
h4 {text-align: center;}
```

text-decoration

Values:

none | [underline || overline || line-through || blink] | inherit

Initial value: none

Applies to: All elements.

Inherited: No.

Computed value: As specified.

Description:

This property allows certain text effects such as underlining. These decorations will span descendant elements that do not have decorations of their own. User agents are not required to support blink. These decorations will span child elements which do not have text decoration defined; see Chapter 6 of *Cascading Style Sheets: The Definitive Guide*, Second Edition (O'Reilly), for more details. Combinations of the values are legal. Any time two text-decoration declarations apply to the same element, the values of the two declarations are *not* combined. For example:

```
h1 {text-decoration: overline;}
h1, h2 {text-decoration: underline;}
```

Given these styles, h1 elements will be underlined with no over-line, because the value of overline completely overrides the value of underline. If h1s should have both overlines and underlines, then use the value overline underline for the h1 rule.

Examples:

```
u {text-decoration: underline;}
.old {text-decoration: line-through;}
u.old {text-decoration: line-through underline;}
```

text-indent

Values:

<length> | <percentage> | inherit

Initial value:	0
Applies to:	Block-level elements.
Inherited:	Yes.
Percentages:	Refer to the width of the containing block.
Computed value:	For percentage values, as specified; for length values, the absolute length.

Description:

Used to define the indentation of the first line of content in a block-level element. This is most often used to create a tab effect. Negative values are permitted and cause outdent (or hanging indent) effects.

Examples:

```
p {text-indent: 5em;}
h2 {text-indent: -25px;}
```

text-transform

Values:

uppercase | lowercase | capitalize | none | inherit

Initial value:	none
Applies to:	All elements.
Inherited:	Yes.
Computed value:	As specified.

Description:

This property changes the case of letters in an element, regardless of the case of the text in the document source. The determination of which letters are to be capitalized by the value capitalize is not precisely defined, as it depends on user agents knowing how to recognize a "word."

Examples:
```
h1 {text-transform: uppercase;}
.title {text-transform: capitalize;}
```

---

top

Values:

<length> | <percentage> | auto | inherit

Initial value: auto

Applies to: Positioned elements (that is, elements for which the value of position is something other than static).

Inherited: No.

Percentages: Refer to the height of the containing block.

Computed value: For relatively positioned elements, see note; for static elements, auto; for length values, the corresponding absolute length; for percentage values, the specified value; otherwise, auto.

Note:

For relatively positioned elements, if both top and bottom are auto, their computed values are both 0; if one of them is auto, it becomes the negative of the other; if neither is auto, bottom will become the negative of the value of top.

Description:

This property defines the offset between the top outer margin edge of a positioned element and the top edge of its containing block.

Examples:
```
#masthead {position: fixed; top: 0;}
sub {position: relative; top: 0.5em; vertical-align:
baseline;}
```

---

unicode-bidi

Values:

normal | embed | bidi-override | inherit

Initial value: normal

Applies to: All elements.

Inherited: No.

Computed value: As specified.

Description:

Allows the author to generate levels of embedding within the Unicode embedding algorithm. User agents that do not support bidirectional text are permitted to ignore this property.

Examples:

```
*:lang(ar) {direction: rtl; unicode-bidi: embed;}
*:lang(es) {direction: ltr; unicode-bidi: normal;}
```

vertical-align

Values:

baseline | sub | super | top | text-top | middle | bottom | text-bottom | <percentage> | <length> | inherit

Initial value: baseline

Applies to: Inline elements and table cells.

Inherited: No.

Percentages: Refer to the value of line-height for the element.

Computed value: For percentage and length values, the absolute length; otherwise, as specified.

Note:

When applied to table cells, only the values `baseline`, `top`, `middle`, and `bottom` are recognized.

Description:

This defines the vertical alignment of an inline element's baseline with respect to the baseline of the line in which it resides. Negative length and percentage values are permitted, and they lower the element instead of raising it. In table cells, this property sets the alignment of the content of the cell within the cell box.

Examples:

```
sup {vertical-align: super;}
.fnote {vertical-align: 50%;}
```

visibility

Values:

visible | hidden | collapse | inherit

Initial value: inherit

Applies to: All elements.

Inherited: No.

Computed value: As specified.

Description:

This specifies whether the element box generated by an element is rendered. This means authors can have the element take up the space it would ordinarily take up while remaining completely invisible. The value `collapse` is used in tables to remove columns or rows from the table's layout.

Examples:

```
ul.submenu {visibility: hidden;}
tr.hide {visibility: collapse;}
```

white-space

Values:

normal | nowrap | pre | pre-wrap | pre-line | inherit

Initial value: normal

Applies to: All elements (CSS2.1); block-level elements (CSS2).

Inherited: No.

Computed value: As specified.

Description:

This declares how whitespace within an element is handled during layout. normal acts like traditional web browsers, in that it reduces any sequence of whitespace to a single space. pre causes whitespace to be treated as it is in the HTML element PRE, with whitespace and returns fully preserved. nowrap prevents an element from line-breaking, as in the "nowrap" attribute for TD and TH elements in HTML4. The values pre-wrap and pre-line were added in CSS2.1; the former causes the user agent to preserve whitespace while still automatically wrapping lines of text, and the latter honors newline characters within the text while collapsing all other whitespace as per normal.

Examples:

```
td {white-space: nowrap;}
tt {white-space: pre;}
```

width

Values:

<length> | <percentage> | auto | inherit

Initial value: auto

Applies to: Block-level and replaced elements.

Inherited:	No.
Percentages:	Refer to the width of the containing block.
Computed value:	For auto and percentage values, as specified; otherwise, an absolute length, unless the property does not apply to the element (then auto).

Description:

This defines the width of an element's content area, outside of which padding, borders, and margins are added. This property is ignored for inline nonreplaced elements. Negative length and percentage values are not permitted.

Examples:

```
table {width: 80%;}
#sidebar {width: 20%;}
.figure img {width: 200px;}
```

word-spacing

Values:

<length> | normal | inherit

Initial value:	normal
Applies to:	All elements.
Inherited:	Yes.
Computed value:	For normal, the absolute length 0; otherwise, the absolute length.

Description:

This defines the amount of whitespace to be inserted between words in an element. For the purposes of this property, a word is defined to be a string of characters surrounded by whitespace. Length values create a modifier to the usual spacing between words; thus, normal is synonymous with 0. Negative length values are permitted and will cause words to bunch closer together.

Examples:

```
p.spacious {word-spacing: 0.5em;}
em {word-spacing: 5px;}
p.cramped {word-spacing: -0.2em;}
```

z-index

Values:

<integer> | auto | inherit

Initial value:	auto
Applies to:	Positioned elements.
Inherited:	No.
Computed value:	As specified.

Description:

This property sets the placement of a positioned element along the z-axis, which is defined to be the axis that extends perpendicular to the display area. Positive numbers are closer to the user, and negative numbers are further away.

Examples:

```
#masthead {position: relative; z-index: 10000;}
```

Tables

border-collapse

Values:

collapse | separate | inherit

Initial value:	separate
Applies to:	Elements with the display value table or table-inline.

Inherited: Yes.

Computed value: As specified.

Note:

In CSS2, the default value was collapse.

Description:

This property is used to define the layout model used in laying out the borders in a table—i.e., those applied to cells, rows, and so forth. Although the property applies only to tables, it is inherited by all the elements within the table.

Examples:

```
table {border-collapse: separate; border-spacing: 3px 5px;}
```

border-spacing

Values:

<length> <length>? | inherit

Initial value: 0

Applies to: Elements with the display value table or table-inline.

Inherited: Yes.

Computed value: Two absolute lengths.

Note:

Property is ignored unless border-collapse value is separate.

Description:

This specifies the distance between cell borders in the separated borders model. The first of the two length values is the horizontal separation and the second is the vertical. This property is ignored unless border-collapse is set to separate. Although the property only applies to tables, it is inherited by all of the elements within the table.

Examples:
```
table {border-collapse: separate; border-spacing: 0;}
table {border-collapse: separate; border-spacing: 3px 5px;}
```

caption-side

Values:
top | bottom

Initial value: top

Applies to: Elements with the display value table-caption.

Inherited: No.

Computed value: As specified.

Note:
The values left and right appeared in CSS2 but were dropped from CSS2.1 due to a lack of widespread support.

Description:
This specifies the placement of a table caption with respect to the table box. The caption is rendered as though it were a block-level element placed just before (or after) the table.

Examples:
```
caption {caption-side: top;}
```

empty-cells

Values:
show | hide | inherit

Initial value: show

Applies to: Elements with the display value table-cell.

| **Inherited:** | Yes. |
| **Computed value:** | As specified. |

Note:

Property is ignored unless border-collapse value is separate.

Description:

This defines the presentation of table cells that contain no content. If shown, the cell's borders and background are drawn. This property is ignored unless border-collapse is set to separate.

Examples:

```
th, td {empty-cells: show;}
```

table-layout

Values:

auto | fixed | inherit

Initial value:	auto
Applies to:	Elements with the display value table or inline-table.
Inherited:	Yes.
Computed value:	As specified.

Description:

This property is used to specify which layout algorithm is used to lay out a table. The fixed layout algorithm is faster but less flexible, while the automatic algorithm is slower but more reflective of traditional HTML tables.

Examples:

```
table.fast {table-layout: fixed;}
```

Paged Media

orphans

Values:
<integer> | inherit

Initial value:	2
Applies to:	Block-level elements.
Inherited:	Yes.
Computed value:	As specified.

Description:

This specifies the minimum number of text lines within the element that can be left at the bottom of a page. This can affect the placement of page breaks within the element.

Examples:

```
p {orhpans: 4;}
ul {orphans: 2;}
```

page-break-after

Values:
auto | always | avoid | left | right | inherit

Initial value:	auto
Applies to:	Nonfloated block-level elements with a position value of relative or static.
Inherited:	No.
Computed value:	As specified.

Description:

This declares whether page breaks should be placed after an element. While it is possible to force breaks with always, it is not possible to guarantee prevention; avoid asks the user agent to avoid inserting a page break if possible.

Examples:

```
div.section {page-break-after: always;}
h2 {page-break-after: avoid;}
```

page-break-before

Values:

auto | always | avoid | left | right | inherit

Initial value: auto

Applies to: Nonfloated block-level elements with a position value of relative or static.

Inherited: No.

Computed value: As specified.

Description:

Declares whether page breaks should be placed before an element. While it is possible to force breaks with always, it is not possible to guarantee prevention; the best an author can do is ask the user agent to avoid inserting a page break if possible.

Examples:

```
p + ul {page-break-before: avoid;}
h2 {page-break-before: always;}
```

page-break-inside

Values:

auto | avoid | inherit

Initial value:	auto
Applies to:	Nonfloated block-level elements with a position value of relative or static.
Inherited:	Yes.
Computed value:	As specified.

Description:

This declares whether page breaks should be placed inside an element. Because an element might be taller than a page box, it is not possible to guarantee prevention; the best an author can do is ask the user agent to avoid inserting a page break if possible.

Examples:

```
table {page-break-inside: avoid;}
```

widows

Values:

<integer> | inherit

Initial value:	2
Applies to:	Block-level elements.
Inherited:	Yes.
Computed value:	As specified.

Description:

This specifies the minimum number of text lines within the element that can be left at the top of a page. This can affect the placement of page breaks within the element.

Examples:

```
p {widows: 4;}
ul {widows: 2;}
```

Dropped from CSS2.1

The following properties appeared in CSS2 but were dropped from CSS2.1 due to a lack of widespread support. They do not have computed value information, since computed values were first explicitly defined in CSS2.1.

Visual Styles

font-size-adjust

Values:

<number> | none | inherit

Initial value: none

Applies to: All elements.

Inherited: Yes.

Description:

The aim of this property is to allow authors to trigger font scaling such that substitute fonts will not look too wildly different from the font the author wanted to use, even if the substituted font has a different x-height. Note that this property does not appear in CSS2.1.

font-stretch

Values:

normal | wider | narrower | ultra-condensed | extra-condensed | condensed | semi-condensed | semi-expanded | expanded | extra-expanded | ultra-expanded | inherit

Initial value: normal

Applies to: All elements.

Inherited: Yes.

Description:

With this property, the character glyphs in a given font can be made wider or narrower, ideally by selected condensed or expanded faces from the font's family. Note that this property does not appear in CSS2.1.

---

marker-offset

Values:

<length> | auto | inherit

Initial value:	auto
Applies to:	Elements with a display value of marker.
Inherited:	No.

Note:

This property is obsolete as of CSS2.1 and will likely not appear in CSS3, with the same holding true for the display value of marker; as of this writing, it appears that other mechanisms will be used to achieve these effects.

Description:

This property specifies the distance between the nearest border edge of a marker box and its associated element box.

---

text-shadow

Values:

none | [<color> || <length> <length> <length>? ,]* [<color> || <length> <length> <length>?] | inherit

Initial value:	none
Applies to:	All elements.
Inherited:	No.

Description:

This permits the assignments of one or more "shadows" to the text in an element. The first two length values in a shadow definition set horizontal and vertical offsets, respectively, from the element's text. The third length defines a blurring radius. Note that this property does not appear in CSS2.1.

Paged Media

marks

Values:

[crop || cross] | none | inherit

Initial value: none

Applies to: Page context.

Inherited: N/A.

Description:

This property defines whether "cross marks" (otherwise known as register marks or registration marks) should be placed outside the content area but within the printable area of the canvas. The exact placement and rendering of the marks is not defined. Note that this value does not appear in CSS2.1.

page

Values:

<identifier> | inherit

Initial value: auto

Applies to: Block-level elements.

Inherited: Yes.

Description:

This property, in conjunction with size, specifies a particular page type to be used in the printing of an element. Note that this property does not appear in CSS2.1.

---

size

Values:

<length>{1,2} | auto | portrait | landscape | inherit

Initial value: auto

Applies to: The page area.

Inherited: No.

Description:

With this property, authors can declare the size and orientation of the page box used in the printing of an element. It can be used in conjunction with page, although this is not always necessary. Note that this property does not appear in CSS2.1.

Aural Styles

---

azimuth

Values:

<angle> | [[left-side | far-left | left | center-left | center | center-right | right | far-right | right-side] || behind] | leftwards | rightwards | inherit

Initial value: center

Applies to: All elements.

Inherited: Yes.

Computed value: Normalized angle.

Description:

This property sets the angle along the horizontal plane (otherwise known as the horizon) from which a sound should seem to emanate. This is used in conjunction with elevation to place the sound at a point on a hypothetical sphere with the user at its center.

---

cue

Values:

[<cue-before> || <cue-after>] | inherit

Initial value: none

Applies to: All elements.

Inherited: No.

Computed value: See individual properties (cue-before, etc.).

Description:

This is a shorthand property that allows an author to define cues that precede and follow the audio rendering of an element's content. A cue is something like an auditory icon.

---

cue-after

Values:

<uri> | none | inherit

Initial value: none

Applies to: All elements.

Inherited: No.

Computed value: For <uri> values, the absolute URI; otherwise, none.

Description:

This property allows an author to define a cue that follows the audio rendering of an element's content.

cue-before

Values:

<uri> | none | inherit

Initial value:	none
Applies to:	All elements.
Inherited:	No.
Computed value:	For <uri> values, the absolute URI; otherwise, none.

Description:

This property allows an author to define a cue that precedes the audio rendering of an element's content.

elevation

Values:

<angle> | below | level | above | higher | lower | inherit

Initial value:	level
Applies to:	All elements.
Inherited:	Yes.
Computed value:	Normalized angle.

Description:

This property sets the angle above or below the horizontal plane (otherwise known as the horizon) from which a sound should seem to emanate. This is used in conjunction with azimuth to place the sound at a point on a hypothetical sphere with the user at its center.

pause

Values:

[[<time> | <percentage>]{1,2}] | inherit

Initial value: 0

Applies to: All elements.

Inherited: No.

Computed value: See individual properties (pause-before, etc.).

Description:

This is a shorthand property that allows an author to define pauses that precede and follow the audio rendering of an element's content. A pause is an interval in which no content is audibly rendered, although background sounds may still be audible.

pause-after

Values:

<time> | <percentage> | inherit

Initial value:s: 0

Applies to: All elements.

Inherited: No.

Computed value: The absolute time value.

Description:

This property allows an author to define the length of a pause that follows the audio rendering of an element's content.

pause-before

Values:

<time> | <percentage> | inherit

Initial value:	0
Applies to:	All elements.
Inherited:	No.
Computed value:	The absolute time value.

Description:

This property allows an author to define the length of a pause that precedes the audio rendering of an element's content.

pitch

Values:

<frequency> | x-low | low | medium | high | x-high | inherit

Initial value:	medium
Applies to:	All elements.
Inherited:	Yes.
Computed value:	The absolute frequency value.

Description:

Specifies the average pitch (frequency) of the speaking voice used to audibly render the element's content. The average pitch of a voice will depend greatly on the voice family.

pitch-range

Values:

<number> | inherit

Initial value:	50
Applies to:	All elements.
Inherited:	Yes.
Computed value:	As specified.

Description:

This property specifies the variation in average pitch used by the speaking voice, while audibly rendering the element's content. The higher the variation, the more animated the voice will sound.

play-during

Values:

<uri> | [mix || repeat]? | auto | none | inherit

Initial value:	auto
Applies to:	All elements.
Inherited:	No.

Computed value:

For <uri> values, the absolute URI; otherwise, as specified.

Description:

This provides a sound to be played in the background while the element's contents are audibly rendered. The sound can be mixed with other background sounds (set using play-during on an ancestor element), or it can replace other sounds for the duration of the element's audio rendering.

richness

Values:

<number> | inherit

| Initial value: | 50 |

Applies to:	All elements.
Inherited:	Yes.
Computed value:	As specified.

Description:

This property sets the brightness of the speaking voice used when audibly rendering the element's content. The brighter the voice, the more it will carry.

---

speak

Values:

normal | none | spell-out | inherit

Initial value:	normal
Applies to:	All elements.
Inherited:	Yes.
Computed value:	As specified.

Description:

This determines how an element's contents will be audibly rendered, or if they will be rendered at all. The value spell-out is typically used for acronyms and abbreviations such as W3C or CSS. If the value is none, then the element is skipped (it takes no time to be audibly rendered).

---

speak-header

Values:

once | always | inherit

Initial value:	once
Applies to:	Elements containing table header information.
Inherited:	Yes.

Computed value: As specified.

Description:

This specifies whether the content of table headers is spoken before every cell associated with those headers, or only when the header associated with a cell is different than the header associated with the previously rendered cell.

speak-numeral

Values:

digits | continuous | inherit

Initial value: continuous

Applies to: All elements.

Inherited: Yes.

Computed value: As specified.

Description:

This property determines how numbers are spoken during audible rendering.

speak-punctuation

Values:

code | none | inherit

Initial value: none

Applies to: All elements.

Inherited: Yes.

Computed value: As specified.

Description:

This property determines how punctuation is spoken during audible rendering. The value code causes punctuation symbols to be rendered literally.

speech-rate

Values:

<number> | x-slow | slow | medium | fast | x-fast | faster| slower | inherit

Initial value:	medium
Applies to:	All elements.
Inherited:	Yes.
Computed value:	An absolute number.

Description:

This sets the average rate at which words are spoken when an element's content is audibly rendered.

stress

Values:

<number> | inherit

Initial value:	50
Applies to:	All elements.
Inherited:	Yes.
Computed value:	As specified.

Description:

This property affects the height of peaks in the intonation of a speaking voice. These peaks are in turn generated by stress marks within a language.

voice-family

Values:

[[<specific-voice> | <generic-voice>],]* [<specific-voice> | <generic-voice>] | inherit

Initial value: User agent–dependent.

Applies to: All elements.

Inherited: Yes.

Computed value: As specified.

Description:

This property is used to define a list of voice families that can be used in the audio rendering of an element's content, and is comparable to font-family. The permitted generic voices are male, female, and child.

volume

Values:

<number> | <percentage> | silent | x-soft | soft | medium| loud | x-loud | inherit

Initial value: medium

Applies to: All elements.

Inherited: Yes.

Computed value: An absolute number.

Description:

This sets the median volume level for the waveform of the audibly rendered content. Thus, a waveform with large peaks and valleys may go well above or below the volume level set with this property. Note that 0 is not the same as silent.

Index

We'd like to hear your suggestions for improving our indexes. Send email to
index@oreilly.com.

Need in-depth answers fast?

O'REILLY NETWORK
Safari® Bookshelf™

Access over 2,000 of the newest and best technology books online

Safari Bookshelf is the premier electronic reference library for IT professionals and programmers—a must-have when you need to pinpoint exact answers in an instant.

Access over 2,000 of the top technical reference books by twelve leading publishers including O'Reilly, Addison-Wesley, Peachpit Press, Prentice Hall, and Microsoft Press. Safari provides the technical references and code samples you need to develop quality, timely solutions.

Try it today with a FREE TRIAL
Visit *www.oreilly.com/safari/max*

For groups of five or more, set up a free, 30-day corporate trial
Contact: *corporate@oreilly.com*

What Safari Subscribers Say:

"The online books make quick research a snap. I usually keep Safari up all day and refer to it whenever I need it."

—Joe Bennett, Sr. Internet Developer

"I love how Safari allows me to access new books each month depending on my needs. The search facility is excellent and the presentation is top notch. It is one heck of an online technical library."

—Eric Winslow, Economist-System, Administrator-Web Master-Programmer

Related Titles Available from O'Reilly

Web Programming

ActionScript Cookbook

ActionScript for Flash MX Pocket Reference

ActionScript for Flash MX: The Definitive Guide, *2nd Edition*

Creating Applications with Mozilla

Dynamic HTML: The Definitive Reference, *2nd Edition*

Flash Remoting: The Definitive Guide

Google Hacks

Google Pocket Guide

HTTP: The Definitive Guide

JavaScript & DHTML Cookbook

JavaScript Pocket Reference, *2nd Edition*

JavaScript: The Definitive Guide, *4th Edition*

PHP 5 Essentials

PHP Cookbook

PHP Pocket Reference, *2nd Edition*

Programming ColdFusion MX, *2nd Edition*

Programming PHP

Web Database Applications with PHP and MySQL, *2nd Edition*

Webmaster in a Nutshell, *3rd Edition*

Web Authoring and Design

Cascading Style Sheets: The Definitive Guide, *2nd Edition*

Dreamweaver MX 2004: The Missing Manual

HTML & XHTML: The Definitive Guide, *5th Edition*

HTML Pocket Reference, *2nd Edition*

Information Architecture for the World Wide Web, *2nd Edition*

Learning Web Design, *2nd Edition*

Web Design in a Nutshell, *2nd Edition*

Web Administration

Apache Cookbook

Apache Pocket Reference

Apache: The Definitive Guide, *3rd Edition*

Essential Blogging

Perl for Web Site Management

Squid: The Definitive Guide

Web Performance Tuning, *2nd Edition*

O'REILLY®

Keep in touch with O'Reilly

1. Download examples from our books

To find example files for a book, go to:
www.oreilly.com/catalog

select the book, and follow the "Examples" link.

2. Register your O'Reilly books

Register your book at *register.oreilly.com*

Why register your books? Once you've registered your O'Reilly books you can:

- Win O'Reilly books, T-shirts or discount coupons in our monthly drawing.
- Get special offers available only to registered O'Reilly customers.
- Get catalogs announcing new books (US and UK only).
- Get email notification of new editions of the O'Reilly books you own.

3. Join our email lists

Sign up to get topic-specific email announcements of new books and conferences, special offers, and O'Reilly Network technology newsletters at:
elists.oreilly.com

It's easy to customize your free elists subscription so you'll get exactly the O'Reilly news you want.

4. Get the latest news, tips, and tools
www.oreilly.com

- "Top 100 Sites on the Web"—PC Magazine
- CIO Magazine's Web Business 50 Awards

Our web site contains a library of comprehensive product information (including book excerpts and tables of contents), downloadable software, background articles, interviews with technology leaders, links to relevant sites, book cover art, and more.

5. Work for O'Reilly

Check out our web site for current employment opportunities:
jobs.oreilly.com

6. Contact us

O'Reilly & Associates
1005 Gravenstein Hwy North
Sebastopol, CA 95472 USA

TEL: 707-827-7000 or 800-998-9938
        (6am to 5pm PST)

FAX: 707-829-0104

order@oreilly.com
    For answers to problems regarding your order or our products.
    To place a book order online, visit:
    www.oreilly.com/order_new

catalog@oreilly.com
    To request a copy of our latest catalog.

booktech@oreilly.com
    For book content technical questions or corrections.

corporate@oreilly.com
    For educational, library, government, and corporate sales.

proposals@oreilly.com
    To submit new book proposals to our editors and product managers.

international@oreilly.com
    For information about our international distributors or translation queries. For a list of our distributors outside of North America check out:
    international.oreilly.com/distributors.html

adoption@oreilly.com
    For information about academic use of O'Reilly books, visit:
    academic.oreilly.com

O'REILLY®

Our books are available at most retail and online bookstores.
To order direct: 1-800-998-9938 • *order@oreilly.com* • *www.oreilly.com*
Online editions of most O'Reilly titles are available at *safari.oreilly.com*